T0078065

# UNCONDITIONAL
# LOVE

## *It's All About Dogs*

DR. GENE W. LARAMY

WESTBOW
PRESS®
A DIVISION OF THOMAS NELSON
& ZONDERVAN

Copyright © 2017 Dr. Gene W. Laramy.
Cover Pictures ©2017 by Brenda Santana

All rights reserved. No part of this book may be used or reproduced by any means, graphic, electronic, or mechanical, including photocopying, recording, taping or by any information storage retrieval system without the written permission of the author except in the case of brief quotations embodied in critical articles and reviews.

This book is a work of non-fiction. Unless otherwise noted, the author and the publisher make no explicit guarantees as to the accuracy of the information contained in this book and in some cases, names of people and places have been altered to protect their privacy.

New Revised Standard Version Bible Copyright © 1989 by the Division of Christian Education of the National Council of the Churches of Christ in the United States of America

Cover pictures are of our seven dogs.

WestBow Press books may be ordered through booksellers or by contacting:

WestBow Press
A Division of Thomas Nelson & Zondervan
1663 Liberty Drive
Bloomington, IN 47403
www.westbowpress.com
1 (866) 928-1240

Because of the dynamic nature of the Internet, any web addresses or links contained in this book may have changed since publication and may no longer be valid. The views expressed in this work are solely those of the author and do not necessarily reflect the views of the publisher, and the publisher hereby disclaims any responsibility for them.

Any people depicted in stock imagery provided by Thinkstock are models, and such images are being used for illustrative purposes only.
Certain stock imagery © Thinkstock.

ISBN: 978-1-5127-6535-9 (sc)
ISBN: 978-1-5127-6537-3 (hc)
ISBN: 978-1-5127-6536-6 (e)

Library of Congress Control Number: 2016919450

Print information available on the last page.

WestBow Press rev. date: 2/27/2017

# CONTENTS

I would like to dedicate this book posthumously to
Byron and Helen Healy,
who were "timeshare parents" to our dog
Rusty.

# FOREWORD

Throughout history there have been individuals who point the way toward a deeper compassion for all life. Dr. Gene W. Laramy is one such individual. In this book *Unconditional Love* he takes the reader from the point when dogs first entered the lives of humans; to when they became part of the family; to when they became service dogs who enhance and save lives.

From childhood we gradually learn and understand the feelings of care and compassion from our parents and others. Ideally, these influences lead us from having these feelings for one another to caring for and having compassion for other creatures.

Where does this awakening often originate in our culture? I find in the chapters of this book the realization that our dogs are frequently catalysts helping us extend our caring and concern for and about other species.

Dr. Laramy's book will fascinate and inspire you as well as provide a deeper understanding of the value of all life.

Ed Boks, Director
Yavapai County Humane Society
Prescott, Arizona

Dogs have been an incredible force through my life and those of many others I know. They bring us much friendship in times of joy and kindheartedness when we are in times of need. The unconditional love given to humans by our canine friends is very meaningful in the people's lives they touch.

As a veterinarian, I see the human-animal relationship each and every day and live the bond with dogs and their people. Dr. Laramy's pets have been my patients for many years. He has always had a profound relationship with his dogs and a deep admiration for who dogs really are and can be.

This book is a journey into the spiritual and personal relationship between humans and dogs. Dr. Laramy writes about how many dogs have shaped his life and his family's lives and how the human-animal bond impacts people more than they believe. He explores some of the biology that makes them unique. He also celebrates the unique and helpful jobs that dogs are capable of handling. After reading this book, you will have a greater appreciation for our canine friends and the human-animal bond, and it may just entice you to start a new relationship with a dog today.

Dr. Kenneth Skinner, DVM
Veterinarian
Prescott Animal Hospital
Prescott, Arizona

# PREFACE

**Unconditional Love**

A newly discovered "chapter" in the book of Genesis has provided the answer to the question "From where do dogs come?"

Adam and Eve said, "Lord, when we were in the garden, you walked with us every day. Now we do not see you anymore. We are lonesome here, and it is difficult for us to remember how much you love us."

And a loud voice said, "No problem! I will create a companion for you that will be with you forever and will be a reflection of my love for you, so you will love me even when you cannot see me. Regardless of how selfish or childish or unlovable you may be, this new companion will accept you as you are and will love you as I do, in spite of yourselves."

And a new animal was created to be a companion for Adam and Eve.

And it was a good animal.

And the new animal was pleased to be with Adam and Eve, and he wagged his tail.

And Adam said, "Lord, I have already named all the animals in the kingdom, and I cannot think of a name for this new animal."

And the voice said, "No problem! Because I have created this new animal to be a reflection of my love for you, his name will be a reflection of my own name, and you will call him Dog."

And Dog lived with Adam and Eve and was a companion to them and loved them unconditionally.

And they were comforted, and God was pleased.

A hypothetical story? Perhaps. *Or is it?*

Though I can't find any theological backing for this story, I firmly believe that *dog* is not only a reflection of the word *God* but is truly a reflection of God's love for us. It is *unconditional* love. We receive it even when we do not deserve it. We receive it as a gift; we cannot earn it.

This leads me to the real reason for writing this book. I believe it is not coincidental that the word *dog* spelled backward is *God*. I firmly believe that dogs are God's messengers to show us the way to live our lives. I know that theologians will have a field day disputing my premise, but I have never seen God's *unconditional love* reflected or expressed as fully as I have through dogs. I most certainly have never experienced that sort of love through human relationships. When you think about it, you can do almost anything to a dog, even be mean to it (which, by the way, I certainly do not condone in any way, shape, or form), and it will still come up to you wagging its tail and licking your hand. I have seen dogs malnourished almost to the point of starvation, and badly treated in other ways too; they still came up to their master with tail wagging and licking their hand. Where else but God can you find this kind of love?

I truly believe that our dogs were sent to us as a blessing from God. I have completed four years of seminary and was in the parish ministry for over forty years, and I must say I have learned as much about the Spirit and *unconditional* love of God and Jesus Christ, as expressed in Galatians 5:22–25, through our dogs as from anyone, anything, or anywhere else.

> The fruit of the spirit is love, joy, peace, patience, kindness, goodness, faithfulness, gentleness, self-control; against such there is no law … If we live by the Spirit, let us walk by the Spirit. Let us have no self-conceit, no provoking one another, no envy of one another. (Galatians 5:22–25)

> A dog is the only thing on earth that will love you more than you love yourself.
> —Josh Billings

**Love:** Since love is a personal relationship, it is not a matter of law and cannot be commanded; and since it is God's own love growing in the hearts of humanity, no one can claim it as a merit for self-salvation.

Likewise, when God incarnates His Spirit in a dog, the love which is the fruit of that Spirit must be the same kind as His own.

However, in every age, especially in times of great pessimism, humanity has found it hard to see how God could have anything in common with humanity, and Christians have been tempted to make a distinction between God's love and human love.

This does not happen with a dog. Dogs' love is as God's love—unconditional, unequivocal, uninvited, and unswerving. Dogs are not tempted to do away with God's love for their own benefit.

All seven of our dogs have possessed this love, always wagging their tails and looking up into one's eyes with a love that is absolutely unexplainable. All a person had to do was to pet them or scratch their ears, and they were friends for life. You just don't find that kind of love in a human being.

> One of the animals which a generous and sociable man would soonest become is a dog. A dog can have a friend; he has affections and character; he can enjoy equally the field and the

fireside; he dreams, he caresses, he propitiates; he offends, and is pardoned; he stands by you in adversity; he is a good fellow.

—Leigh Hunt

**Joy:** With all of our dogs it has been a joy to come home and have them meet us at the door with tail wagging and running all around the house as happy as they could be that we were home with them once again. This took place whether we were gone for five minutes or a whole day. It was their way of letting us know how happy and full of joy they were that we were home.

One of our dogs, Rusty, was a perfect example of a dog that could be sorrowful for one reason or another, but at the same time be full of joy and rejoicing. He would hang his head and give us a very sad look if we were going to leave the house and not take him with us, but upon our return it was as if nothing had changed. He would always meet us with the same cheerful greeting. It was sort of ironic that the only time of the week he would not let us know he was unhappy was when we were leaving without him on Sunday morning for church. Come to think of it, I believe all of our dogs have acted in the same way.

Dogs are our link to paradise. They don't know evil or jealousy or discontent. To sit with a dog on a hillside on a glorious afternoon is to be back in Eden, where doing nothing was not boring—it was peace.

—Milan Kundera

**Peace:** As long as we were with any of our dogs, they were content and full of peace. Usually they would be curled up on the floor by my feet, or, in the case of Cassie, she would be lying in Inez's lap, sometimes fast asleep, other times wide awake, but always the epitome of peace and contentment. All of them would extend that feeling of peace to both of us, which in turn would make us have a feeling of total contentment and peace.

Dogs never talk about themselves but listen to you as you talk about yourself, and keep up an appearance of being interested in the conversation.

—Jerome K. Jerome

**Patience:** Many times throughout the Bible, God asks us to be patient. Inez put a little plaque on my desk several years ago that reads, "Dear God, give me patience, and I want it right now." I am probably the most impatient person in the world. When I want something done, I want it done right now. When I want to buy something, I want it yesterday. However, I am improving, only because our dogs have taught me a lesson. Shotzy is still teaching me.

All of our dogs have shown a lot of patience, but the one we have now, Shotzy, is the most patient dog I have ever been around. She is definitely showing me one thing that I lack—patience. Even in the morning when she has to go outside to do her duty, she patiently stands by the door while I put on my coat and cap and finally open the door. When we are on our walk along the lake and meet people along the way and I stop to talk, she will either sit or lie down while we are talking. She never seems to be in a hurry to get going. I am learning from her; really, I am.

> Near this spot are deposited the remains of one who possessed Beauty without Vanity, Strength without Insolence, Courage without Ferocity, and the Virtues of Man without his vices. This praise, which would be unmeaning Flattery, if inscribed over human ashes, is but a just Tribute to the memory of BOTSWAIN, a dog.
>
> —John Cam Hobhouse

**Kindness:** Of course God exudes kindness, as does his Son, Jesus the Christ. Dogs, if given the chance and the right kind of love, will also exude this same kindness. All of our dogs have been very kind to all who have come in contact with them—wagging their tail, licking a person's hand, and all in all showing kindness to stranger and friend alike. We always tell people when we meet them for the first time to approach the dog with their hand under the dog's chin. As long as dogs can see your hand, they will not be afraid and feel threatened or react in a mean way. I personally believe there is no such thing as a mean dog. They have to be taught meanness by a mean master.

> The gift I am sending you is called a dog, and is in fact, the most precious and valuable possession of mankind.
>
> —Theodorus Gaza

**Goodness:** Like God, all of our dogs have always been good and sincere. They have let us know in no uncertain terms they loved us no matter what. Their love and devotion has been as sincere as it could possibly have been. If we took a walk in the rain, even though most of our dogs did not like water, they never complained. All of them have wanted to be wherever we were no matter what. It's probably a combination of knowing we loved them and wanted them to be with us, and their being there to protect us from all harm.

> He is your friend, your partner, your defender, your dog. You are his life, his love, his leader. He will be yours, faithful and true, to the last beat of his heart. You owe it to him to be worthy of such devotion.
>
> —Anonymous

**Faithfulness:** Another lesson from God is that He is dependable and is always there when we need Him or call upon Him. Other attributes dogs have, like God, are faithfulness and loyalty. Whenever we are in trouble of any kind, all we have to do is ask God to help us and He is right there beside us.

The same thing has been true with our dogs. All we have had to do is ask them to come to our side and they would do so immediately. Dogs are extremely loyal to their masters, and if you happen to be away from them for an extended length of time, when you come back it is as if you never left. They are that loyal. There has never been a day that our dogs haven't expressed their faithfulness and loyalty toward us. They always have been by the door when we've returned from being away, ready to greet us with the wag of a tail and a lick on the hand. When people would visit, the dogs would circle around and greet everyone, but then they would come and lie down next to me or Inez. They would let everyone know, these are the people to whom they are totally committed. There are times when I have felt down and sort of blue. They seem to be able to sense that and will come over and lay their head on my leg as if to say, "It's okay, Dad. I am here if you need me." Not long ago, I went into our bedroom and sat down at my desk to take care of some things. I sat on the chair the wrong way, the chair went out from under me, and I fell to the floor. Shotzy was lying on her "perch" (an old sofa we designated as her place to lie), and when she heard the commotion in the bedroom, she was immediately by my side, licking my face and cuddling as tightly as she could against my body. She was there before Inez could come from the kitchen to see what was going on.

I have heard of several instances when a person has fallen or been hurt outside, and their dog would lie down next to them and protect them from all who tried to approach, even to the point sometimes of not letting people help. They are there to protect and soothe their guardian no matter what.

I recently read in the paper about a man who went back into his burning house to save his dog. Unfortunately, the man died in his effort. Some would say he was foolish to risk his life for just a dog. But I can certainly understand, because loyalty goes both ways, and his dog was a member of his family. I would do the same thing. God has shown us that to be loyal is to be godly.

This is what we have found with all the dogs we have owned. They have been as dependable and loyal as anyone or anything could possibly be.

All our dogs have been very protective of us, and they've always been there for us if we needed them. Shotzy is carrying on this tradition. She is extremely protective and loyal. She is usually either on her perch or lying next to me wherever I may be, or whatever I may be doing.

> Histories are more full of examples of the fidelity of dogs
> than of friends.
>
> —Alexander Pope

I am a firm believer that if any person will be kind to a dog, they will find that same loyalty, love, kindness, goodness, patience, joy, faithfulness, gentleness, and self-control we have experienced in our seven dogs. It bothers me to no end to see people who have a dog and never let it inside the house. They are staked or penned outside regardless of the weather, are very seldom ever spoken to, and are almost completely ignored by their owners. What is the sense of having a dog if that is the way people are going to treat them? It is beyond my comprehension how anyone can treat these magnificent animals in a cruel way. This is what can make a dog mean.

# ACKNOWLEDGMENTS

I wouldn't have been able to write this book
without the encouragement, love, and confidence of my dear wife,
Inez.
Thank you, darling, from the bottom of my heart.

And, of course, this book could not have been written
if not for the *unconditional love* of our dear friends and companions:

Duke
Tuffy
Ginger
Spicy
Rusty
Cassie
Shotzy

Thank you, dogs, for being a huge part of our lives and giving us *unconditional love.*

## CHAPTER 1

# Dogs: An Overview

**Gray Wolf**

As far as I could find out, the domestic dog is a subspecies of the gray wolf, a member of the Canidae family of the mammalian order Carnivora. The dog was the first domesticated animal, as far as we know, and it has been the most widely working, hunting, and companion animal in human history.

Evidence shows an evolutionary split between the modern dog's lineage and the modern wolf's lineage that took place perhaps around one hundred thousand years ago. Another recent study supports claims of dog domestication between fourteen thousand and sixteen thousand years ago, with a range between nine thousand and thirty-four thousand years ago, depending on mutation rate assumptions. I believe, from all my research, no one really knows how long dogs have existed, but suffice it to say, they have been around for a long, long time.

Dogs perform many roles for people, such as hunting, herding, pulling loads, protecting, assisting police and military personnel, companionship, and, more recently, aiding handicapped individuals (more about this later). This impact on human society has given them the nickname "man's best friend" in the Western world. And I, for one, can certainly attest to that.

To be sure, the inherited complex behavior of domesticated dogs comes from their wolf ancestors, who would have been pack hunters with complex body language. The domestication of dogs may have been one of the key forces that led to human success. Sophisticated forms of social cognition and communication may account for their training ability, playfulness, and ability to fit into human households and social situations, and these attitudes have given dogs a relationship with humans that has enabled them to become one of the most successful species on the planet today.

I would imagine wolves and their dog descendants would have derived significant benefit from living in human camps, as there would be more safety and a more reliable food supply. They would have benefited from the upright gait of humans, which gives them a larger range over which to see potential predators and prey, as well as a color vision that, at least by day, gives humans better visual discrimination. Humans would also have derived enormous benefit from the dogs associated with the camps. For instance, dogs would have improved sanitation by cleaning up food scraps. Dogs may also have provided warmth, as referred to in the expression "three-dog night" (an exceptionally cold night); in other words, it took three dogs to keep the person warm. They also would have alerted the camp to the presence of predators or strangers, using their acute hearing to provide an early warning.

But the most significant benefit perhaps would have been the use of the sensitive senses of smell, sight, and hearing of dogs to assist with the hunt. The relationship between the presence of a dog and success in the hunt is often mentioned as the primary reason for the domestication of the wolf. Studies that have shown hunter groups with and without dogs give quantitative support to the hypothesis that the benefit of cooperative hunting was an important factor in wolf domestication.

The coming together of dogs and humans would have greatly improved the chances of survival for humans, and the domestication of dogs may have been one of the key forces that led to human success.

# CHAPTER 2

# Bonding between Humans and Dogs

The most widespread form of interspecies bonding occurring between humans and dogs and the keeping of dogs as companions have a long history. Pet populations grew significantly after World War II. When I was a kid, which was many years ago, dogs were kept outside more often than they are today. Why? I will never know, but they still served in many critical areas: acting as a guard, children's playmate, or walking companion. Since the 1980s, there have been changes in the role of the pet dog, such as increased role of dogs and the emotional support of their human guardians. People and dogs have become increasingly integrated and implicated in each other's lives, to the point that pet dogs actively shape the way a family and home are experienced. Dogs have literally become members of the family.

It takes a considerable amount of work and time to transform a pet dog into an ideal companion. The list of goods, services, and places available to help do this is enormous: from furniture and housing to dog groomers, therapists, trainers, and caretakers. While dog training as an organized activity can be traced back to the eighteenth century, in the last decades of the twentieth century it became a high-profile issue, as many normal dog behaviors, such as barking, jumping up, digging, rolling in dung, fighting, and urine marking became increasingly incompatible with the new role of a pet dog. Dog training books, classes, and television programs proliferated as the process of developing the pet dog continued.

The majority of contemporary people with dogs describe their pet as a big part of the family, as well they should be. Dogs play an active role in family life; for example, family members talk to their dogs oftentimes like they would talk to other humans: "What do you want to do today?" "Do you want to go for a walk; go for a ride?" "What do you want for supper?" etc.

Many dogs also have set tasks or routines as family members, the most common of which are bringing in the newspaper from the lawn, barking when someone is coming to the door, or watching and guarding the kids when they are playing outdoors. Increasingly, human family members engage in activities centered on the perceived needs and interests of the dog or in which the dog is an integral partner.

I read somewhere that about 77.5 million people have dogs in the United States. I'm not sure what that number really is, but living in dog-friendly Prescott, Arizona, I can believe it is at least that many. Yet although several programs promote pet adoption, a very small percentage of the owned dogs come from a shelter. This is extremely sad, as I understand over 1.5 million of these amazing animals are euthanized every year in the United States because they can't find homes. What a shame. What a waste. What a bad commentary on people's lack of compassion.

There does not seem to be any gender preference among dogs as pets, as the statistical data reveal an equal number of female and male dog pets. Dogs have lived and worked with humans in so many roles that they have earned that unique nickname, "man's best friend." This is true because they exemplify unconditional love to their owner and the owner's family. They have been bred for herding livestock, hunting, rodent control, guarding, helping fishermen with nets, detecting danger, and pulling loads, in addition to their role as companions. They have also been trained as seeing-eye dogs for the blind, as helpers to those who are deaf, and as therapy dogs, as well as for many more tasks that will be covered in the next chapter.

## CHAPTER 3

# Service and Companion Dogs

Service dogs—such as guide dogs, utility dogs, assistant dogs, hearing dogs, and psychological therapy dogs—provide assistance to individuals with physical or mental disabilities. For example, some dogs owned by epileptics have been known to alert their handler when the handler shows signs of an impending seizure, sometimes well in advance of the onset. The advance notice allows the handler to seek safety, medication, or medical care.

The scientific evidence is mixed as to whether the companionship of a dog can enhance human physical health and psychological well-being. I have read studies suggesting there are benefits to both, which I personally believe is true from my own observations. However, some of these studies have been criticized for being poorly controlled and finding that the health of elderly people is related to their health habits and social supports but not to their ownership of, or attachment to, a companion animal. But earlier studies have shown that people who keep pet dogs or cats exhibit better mental and physical health than those who do not, making fewer visits to the doctor and being less likely to be on medication than nonguardians. I am a firm believer that owning a pet prolongs a person's life, and I find that in my own experience, owning dogs has kept a tendency for high blood pressure in check. Our dogs have had a considerable calming effect on me.

Studies also have pointed to significantly less absenteeism from school because of sickness among children who live with pets. In one study, new guardians reported a highly significant reduction in minor health problems during the first month following pet acquisition.

In addition, people with pet dogs engage in considerably more physical exercise than those with cats and those without pets. Inez and I walk our dog, Shotzy, every morning, and we would probably not be as diligent in walking if we did not have her. I know it has made a considerable difference in my well-being. Perhaps people without pets will exhibit no statistically significant changes in health or behavior, but I know what having a dog has done for us. This, to me, provides evidence that keeping pets absolutely has positive effects on human health and behavior, and for guardians of dogs, these effects are relatively long-term. Pet guardianship has also been associated with fewer heart problems, perhaps because guardians obtain more exercise. Further studies have shown that pet owners are significantly less likely to die within one year of acute myocardial infarction than those who do not own dogs.

The health benefits of dogs can result from contact with dogs in general and not solely from having dogs as pets. For example, when in the presence of a pet dog, people show reductions in cardiovascular, behavioral, and psychological indicators of anxiety. The benefits of contact with a dog also include social support, as dogs are able to not only provide companionship and social support themselves but also to act as facilitators of social interactions between humans. For example, wheelchair users experience more positive social interactions with strangers when they are accompanied by a dog than when they are not.

We have a "Courthouse Square" in Prescott, Arizona, where literally hundreds of residents walk their dogs every day. This is a place where many residents, with or without dogs, congregate, visit, pet other dogs, communicate with the animals, and just have a fine experience. This has to be a healthy endeavor, as they forget the trials of the world as they communicate with their dog or with other dogs. And if people do not have dog, they communicate with other peoples' dogs. This also allows them an excuse to get out of the house and interact with others.

## CHAPTER 4

# The Differences between Dogs and Humans

**Sight:** It doesn't take a Philadelphia lawyer to know that a dog has tremendous eyesight. In the morning when we take our dog, Shotzy, for a walk along the lake down below our home, she can spot a neighbor walking his dog coming toward us way before we can even make them out. She gets very excited, as she knows our neighbor will have a treat for her when we meet on the path.

All of our dogs have had great eyesight, much better than ours. They can see a rabbit or some other animal in the weeds long before we can spot them. This always amazes me, but not as much as it does my wife, who is usually leading our animal; they dart one way or another because they have seen a bunny in the weeds, pulling Inez along with them. She says her left arm is longer than her right arm just from being yanked by Shotzy.

**Hearing:** Likewise, a dog's hearing is much more acute than a human's. All of our dogs have had very good hearing. However, two of them have gone deaf in their later years, probably from the television being too loud, or my shrill whistle, or from other loud noises. Shotzy can hear someone coming up to the front door long before we even know anyone is around. She can also hear and distinguish our car long before we get to the house, and, according to our pet sitter, Shotzy gets all excited because we are coming home. Have you ever watched dogs when they seem to be hearing something? Their ears swivel all over. It has been said dogs have eighteen or more muscles that can tilt, rotate, raise, or lower a dog's ear, which gives them better ways to hear. A dog can identify a sound's location much faster than a human can, as well as hear sounds coming from a greater distance away.

**Smell:** Dogs' sense of smell is also far more acute than that of humans. It has been estimated that dogs have 125 to 220 million smell-sensitive receptors, which means their sense of smell ranges around 100 million times greater than that of humans. This capability explains why they can detect bombs buried in the dirt, drugs hidden behind metal parts of cars, or even whether a person has cancer just by smelling his or her breath. This is fascinating, if not almost unbelievable.

Again, when we walk Shotzy, she will have her nose in the air detecting a coyote or a javelina somewhere in the vicinity, and sure enough, we will soon see one bounding along through the weeds. She warned us one day before we came around a corner only to be faced with nine javelinas in a row. These animals are nothing to be friendly with, as they can be quite vicious and have teeth like razors.

These examples show how fantastic dogs really are. Besides, they display unconditional love to their handlers.

## CHAPTER 5

# So What Can Dogs Do That People Can't?

1.  Dogs can smell roadside bombs for the military. People can't.
2.  Dogs can sniff out illegal drugs no matter how well people think they have them camouflaged. People can't.
3.  Dogs can tell when a person is going to have a seizure way before the event happens. People can't.
4.  Dogs can tell when a person has cancer just by smelling his or her breath. People can't.
5.  Dogs can be trained to be seeing-eye dogs for the blind.

When I was working on my doctorate degree in San Anselmo, California, I visited Guide Dogs for the Blind facilities in San Rafael, California. This was an amazing experience. The following are some of the things I learned while talking to the trainers.

Established in 1942, Guide Dogs for the Blind is the largest guide dog school in the United States. Services are provided to students from the United States and Canada at no cost to them. Guide Dogs for the Blind breeds Labrador retrievers, golden retrievers, and Lab/golden mixes from their own stock, selected for temperament, intelligence, and health. When I visited, they also had a number of German shepherds.

They also explained about people whom they call "raisers" in the nine western states (Arizona, California, Oregon, Colorado, Idaho, Nevada, Utah, Texas, and Washington) who raise the puppies for Guide Dogs for the Blind. When I was there, they had more than 1,400 puppy-raising families in these western states. The puppies do not belong to the puppy raisers, but instead are loaned to them when they are between eight and ten weeks of age. The puppy raisers work with these dogs, teaching them basic obedience commands, for about one year before returning them to Guide Dogs for the Blind for formal training. If the dogs have not already been neutered or spayed, they are screened as potential breeders before they go into formal training. They also sometimes exchange breeders with other schools, both nationally and internationally, to ensure sufficient diversity in the gene pool. Breeders are placed with families who are local to Guide Dogs' San Rafael campus.

Returned dogs then go through formal training, which is an eight-phase program. Any person who is blind or visually impaired, desiring enhanced mobility and independence, can benefit from the skills a guide dog provides. The person must be legally blind, able to travel independently, and suited to work with a dog. Typically, six to eight students take part in each of the two-week training classes.

Dogs that are not suitable for guide dog work due to health, behavior, or age issues are dropped from training and are described as "career changed." Around 50 percent of all dogs that go through the program are career changed. Career-changed dogs can be adopted as pets by their puppy raisers. Many dogs also go on to have other careers, such as search and rescue dogs or dogs for diabetics.

Guide Dogs for the Blind also has a K9 Buddy program in which K9 buddies are dogs that are not suited for guide dog work and are placed as pets with visually impaired children This program gives the children not only companionship but also the opportunity to learn to care for a dog. This experience helps prepare them for the responsibilities involved with having a guide dog someday. One of the most interesting things I learned at the school was that before a trainer can turn a dog over to a blind person, he or she must go with the dog to downtown San Francisco, be blindfolded, and then let the dog lead him or her around the streets. This is a sort of a graduation ceremony in which the trainer must show faith that he or she has trained the dog well.

### 6. Dogs can be trained to be hearing dogs.

These dogs are trained to alert people to household sounds that are necessary for everyday safety and independence. They are trained to make physical contact and lead their person to the source of the sound. By providing sound awareness and companionship, these dogs increase employability and provide greatly increased freedom and independence.

Many people are curious about what hearing dogs can do for people who are deaf or hard of hearing when they are in public. The most important thing a hearing dog provides a person in public is an increased awareness of his or her environment. A hearing dog isn't specifically trained to alert to sounds in public, such as a siren or a honking horn. However, when a person who is deaf or hard of hearing takes his or her hearing dog into public areas, he or she will gain an awareness of the environment by paying attention to what the hearing dog is reacting to. When the dog turns to look at something it hears, the person will notice and turn to see what's happening as well.

As far as training goes, at Dogs for the Deaf, it generally takes four to six months for evaluation of temperament, obedience training, socialization, and sound training. The dogs are taught to work for toys and affection.

They train their hearing dogs to respond to seven different sounds: fire and smoke alarms, the telephone, oven timer, alarm clock, doorbell/door knock, and name call (and sometimes the baby cry). Of course once placed with their deaf partner, the dogs easily learn to respond to additional sounds, such as the microwave oven, teakettle, and washer/dryer. Hearing dogs can be taught to alert people to any repetitive sound that can be set up and practiced regularly. If the sound is inconsistent or too difficult to set up and practice, it is hard for the dog to learn to work it.

When the hearing dog is ready for placement with an approved applicant, the trainer travels to the client's home for one-on-one training with the client and all family members. Placement training is generally three to five days in length.

Dogs for the Deaf provides follow-up training for the life of the team. Follow-up training includes guidance and suggestions through verbal contact, written contact, and in-home visits.

The contact information is as follows:

Dogs for the Deaf
10175 Wheeler Road
Central Point, Oregon 97502
Phone: 1-800-990-DOGS (3047)

One of the things I am very impressed with is that all the dogs used with Dogs for the Deaf are rescue dogs and will never be returned to the kennel.

### 7. Dogs can be trained to be autism assistance dogs.[1]

Dogs for the Deaf also trains autism assistance dogs for children and families living with autism. The rise in autism rates is staggering. The evolution of programs geared toward the successful integration of children with autism into routine daily activities includes autism assistance dogs.

Autism assistance dogs are trained to enhance the safety of children on the autism spectrum. The dog can have a calming effect on the child, increasing the child's willingness and ability to communicate. They can help to improve the child's social skills and reduce behavior common to children on the autism spectrum. Autism assistance dogs can also have a stabilizing force, keeping the child out of traffic, bodies of water, and other dangerous situations. The training for these dogs generally takes four to six months.

Unfortunately, the company is revamping their program at the present time, so they have suspended it for the immediate future. They hope to have it up and running and expect to begin placing autism dogs again in the next year or so.

### 8. Dogs can be trained to be therapy dogs.[2]

A therapy dog is a dog trained to provide comfort to people in hospitals, retirement homes, nursing homes, schools, hospices, and disaster areas, and to people with learning difficulties.

A small dog named Smoky was found in a New Guinea jungle foxhole in March 1944 by an American soldier. The soldier then sold the dog to Cpl. William A. Wynne for two Australian pounds. Smoky spent the next eighteen months moving about in a backpack, and going on combat flights with Cpl. Wynne, who served in the 26th Photo Reconnaissance Squadron of the Fifth Army Air Force. During this time Smoky also learned to parachute from a tree. Smoky became a hero in January 1945 when, on Luzon Island in the Philippines, she helped engineers lay a teletype wire beneath a seventy-foot-wide airstrip. Smoky was placed into an eight-inch-diameter pipe that lay under the airstrip, with a kite string tied to her collar so that a telephone line could be attached to it and delivered to the other side of the airstrip. Cpl. Wynne called the dog from the farthest end of the pipe, and despite darkness and many blockages of sand and soil, leaving her with only a few inches of headroom, Smoky was able to achieve this feat within two minutes. Her efforts turned what would otherwise have been a dangerous three-day exercise into one taking only several minutes; and it left the airfield open, saving 40 planes and 250 ground crew personnel from exposure to enemy fire.

When Cpl. Wynne entered a New Guinea hospital with dengue fever, nurses took Smoky on their rounds with them, and Smoky became the "first therapy dog on record."

Dr. Charles Mayo, of the Mayo Clinic, who was the commanding officer of the hospital, also bent the rules and allowed Smoky to sleep with his master, Bill, on his hospital bed.

Smoky worked with wounded soldiers, helping many to cope with the terrible injuries they had received and the horrific sights they had seen, in what today is recognized as battlefield PTSD (post-traumatic stress disorder). Smoky served at the US Hundred and Ninth Fleet Hospital and at the 42nd General Hospital in Brisbane, Australia.

Smoky went on to be credited with twelve combat missions, and she was awarded eight battle stars. She entered the United States in a specially designed flight oxygen mask carrying case, and she went to live and work with Bill in Cleveland, Ohio. Often known as "Yorkey Doodle Dandy," the title of William A. Wynne's book, Smoky spent the rest of her life as a medical therapy dog visiting hospitals, nursing homes, and orphanages.

Six monuments have been dedicated to Smoky throughout the United States, and two have been dedicated in Australia. Smoky passed away in 1957 at the age of fourteen and was laid to rest in the Cleveland Metroparks in Ohio. William A. Wynne resides in central Ohio.

The RSPCA Australian Purple Cross Award was established in 1993 to recognize the deeds of animals that have shown outstanding service to humans, particularly where they have demonstrated exceptional courage, by risking their own safety or life, to save a person from injury or death. Since its inception, only nine animals have been awarded this prestigious award. Smoky received this award on Friday, December 11, 2015.

**Smoky**

The systematic use of therapy dogs is attributed to a woman who worked as a registered nurse. This woman noticed how well patients responded to visits by a chaplain and his golden retriever. In 1976, she started a program for training dogs to visit institutions. Other health care professionals noticed the therapeutic effects of animal companionship, such as relieving stress, lowering blood pressure, and raising mood, and the demand for therapy dogs continued to grow. In recent years, therapy dogs have been enlisted to help children overcome speech and emotional disorders.

In 1982, another woman, Nancy Stanley, founded Tender Loving Zoo, a nonprofit organization that introduced animal therapy to severely disabled children and convalescent hospitals for the elderly. She got the idea while working at the Los Angeles Zoo, where she noticed how disabled visitors responded eagerly to the animals. She researched the beneficial effects that animals can have on patients and began taking her pet toy poodle, Freeway, to the Revere Developmental Center for the severely disabled.

Inspired by the response of the patients and the encouragement of the staff, she bought a van, recruited helpers, and persuaded a pet store to lend animals. Soon requests for TLZ visits were coming from schools, hospitals, and convalescent homes throughout the country. Partly as a result of this woman's work, the concept of dog therapy has broadened to "animal-assisted therapy" or "pet therapy," including many other species, such as therapy cats, therapy rabbits, and therapy birds.[3]

One example of the use of therapy dogs is in building self-confidence. Many children have difficulty reading. As a result, they can develop low self-esteem while reading in public. By reading to a dog, children relax and focus on the dog and the reading, therefore building self-confidence.

Therapy dogs are usually not service or assistant dogs but can be if designated as such for people with post-traumatic stress disorder. These service dogs perform tasks for persons with disabilities and have a legal right to accompany their owners in most areas. In the United States, service dogs are legally protected at the federal level by the Americans with Disabilities Act of 1990. Regular therapy dogs are not trained to assist specific individuals and do not qualify as service dogs under the Americans with Disability Act. Institutions may invite, limit, or prohibit access by therapy dogs. If the dogs are allowed, many institutions have rigorous requirements for them.

Many organizations provide evaluation and registration for therapy dogs. In the United States, some organizations require that a dog pass the equivalent of the American Kennel Club's Canine Good Citizen test and then add further requirements specific to the environments in which the dog will be working. Other organizations have their own testing requirements. Typical tests might ensure that a dog can handle sudden and loud or strange noises; can walk on assorted unfamiliar surfaces comfortably; are not frightened by people with canes, wheelchairs, or an unusual style of walking or moving; get along well with children and with the elderly; and so on.

Colleges and universities in the United States bring therapy dogs to campus to help students de-stress.

Therapy Dogs Incorporated is a national organization with its corporate offices located in Cheyenne, Wyoming. It was incorporated in 1990, and it currently has over twelve thousand handler/dog teams in the United States, Canada, Puerto Rico, and the US territories.

It is a goal of Therapy Dogs Incorporated to provide registration, support, and insurance for members who are involved in volunteer animal-assisted activities. These activities include, but are not limited to, visits to hospitals, special needs centers, schools, and nursing homes. Their objective is to form a network of caring individuals who are willing to share their special animals in order to bring happiness and cheer to people, young and old alike.

We have a therapy dog group in Prescott, and they say most therapy dogs are personal pets who meet certain requirements of good manners and good health, and pass testing and evaluations.

Here in Prescott, as well as in other places, therapy dogs must do the following:

- Be at least one year of age
- Have good disposition around other dogs
- Listen to their handlers
- Allow strangers to touch them all over
- Not jump on people when interacting
- Walk on a leash without pulling
- Not mind strange noises and smells
- Be calm during petting
- Not be afraid of people walking unsteadily
- Be current on all vaccines required by local laws
- Have a negative fecal test every twelve months
- Be clean and well groomed

I was in the hospital for surgery recently, and I was visited by a legally blind person with his therapy dog. I must say, he made my day by coming over to my bed, ready to be petted. I am not sure what breed of dog he was, but he looked like some kind of spaniel.

Any dog of any breed, or mixed breeds with the qualifications listed above, is a good candidate to be a therapy dog. The membership process involves the handler/dog team passing the handling portion of the test followed by three successful supervised visits in the field.[4]

Being a minister, I have made many calls on people in hospitals and nursing homes and have observed firsthand the workings of therapy dogs. I've seen children in cancer wards who "light up like a Christmas tree" when a therapy dog comes in and they begin to play with it. I have seen Alzheimer's patients who will not, or cannot, speak to anyone or have any connection with them but will reach down and pet a therapy dog and talk to it. I've seen people lying in bed with a therapy dog lying next to them, and they are petting the dog with a big smile on their faces. I have seen people who have suffered strokes and cannot speak, reach down and pet a therapy dog and have a big smile on their faces while doing so. If you want to see the importance of a therapy dog, take a stroll through the Shriners Children's Cancer Hospital. Kids respond especially well with the dogs. From my standpoint, to sum it up in one statement: *therapy dogs are priceless.* They are the epitome of unconditional love that spreads that love to all with whom they come in contact.

If you wish to get in touch with the Alliance of Therapy Dogs., you may do so by typing that name in Google Search.

## 9. Dogs can be trained to be search and rescue dogs.

Search and rescue dogs are trained in many different ways, but all use their highly sensitive sense of smell to search for people. They have been used to find people caught in avalanches (e.g., St. Bernards); to find lost children; to find people who have wandered away from nursing homes; to help track down criminals who are on the run; and to find people buried in collapsed buildings, mud slides, or other catastrophes such as the 9/11 disaster ... which I will say more about later. They also are trained to find cadavers. Dogs can be trained to do all of these things, but people can't. They truly are amazing animals.

Perhaps the most recent and most publicized event where rescue dogs were used is the 9/11 implosion of the World Trade Center towers in New York City. Over three hundred search and rescue teams showed up at the site. Unfortunately, very few people were found, which caused both the dogs and their handlers much stress. However, some people were saved, which, in my mind, made it very worthwhile.

I read about a woman who was working in her office in one of the World Trade Center towers when she heard a terrible noise outside. As she raced down the stairs, she felt the building collapse around her. Twenty-seven hours later, she would be the final living person rescued from the rubble at Ground Zero. She was not found by a human equipped with special gear. Instead, her savior had four legs and lots of fur—a rescue dog.

Though there were a number of survivors, many were too shaken to tell their stories, but this woman said she wanted to tell her story because she had a mission to fulfill, as she had been saved.

She said, "It was dark, and everything was rumbling. Pinned under cement and steel and unable to move, I prayed and asked God to help me." She went on to say, "It was so awesome that the dogs could have this kind of sense, to find people buried under the rubble. I felt a totally renewed life in me ... that was the most joyful moment." Although doctors told her she would never walk again, she defied all odds and now not only walks but runs.

Another incredible story about a dog's love on 9/11 involves Michael Hingson, a blind World Trade Center employee who was led safely out of the building by his trusted canine companion, a yellow Labrador retriever named Roselle.[6] Hingson remembers encountering firefighters on his way out of the building. One of them stopped to pet Roselle and cuddle her, even though guide dogs aren't supposed to be petted. Still, Hingson doesn't regret it, because "It was probably the last unconditional act of love he got," Hingson said about this fireman, who was killed that day in the line of duty.

You can read more of Hingson's incredible experience in his wonderful book *Thunder Dog: The True Story of a Blind Man, His Guide Dog and the Triumph of Trust at Ground Zero.* Afterward, Hingson became public affairs director for a seeing-eye dog organization. Roselle traveled the world with him until she died at the age of thirteen.

Roselle was honored as the first recipient of the American Humane Association (not to be confused with the Humane Society of the United States) Hero Dog Award. Four hundred thousand votes were cast in the online poll that determined the winner. Unfortunately, Roselle passed away several months before the winner was announced. The grand prize for the American Humane Association Hero Dog Award is ten thousand dollars, which is given to a charity that reflects the contributions of the animal. The award was given on November 11, 2011.

Another story going around was about a dog named Daisy who led his blind master out of the building from several stories up. The story states that he also went back into the building and rescued many more people. However, this story proved to be false.

Michael Hingson and His Dog, Roselle

**St Bernards**

Perhaps the most famous, and most thought of when the term *rescue dog* is mentioned, is the St. Bernard. The St. Bernard is a breed of very large working dogs from the Italian and Swiss Alps. The St. Bernard is a giant dog. The weight of the breed is generally between 140 and 264 pounds or more, and the height at the withers is between 27 ½ inches and 35 ½ inches. Their coat can be either smooth or rough, with the smooth coat close and flat. The rough coat is dense but flat, and it is more profuse around the neck and legs. The coat is typically a red color with white, or sometimes a mahogany brindle with white. Black shading is usually found on the face and ears. The tail is long and heavy, hanging low. The eyes have naturally tight lids. They are actually very impressive and beautiful animals.

The earliest written records of the St. Bernard breed are from monks at the hospice located at the Great St. Bernard Pass, with paintings and drawings of the dog dating even earlier.

The Great St. Bernard Hospice is a hospice or hostel for travelers in Switzerland. It is located at almost nine thousand feet altitude at the Great St. Bernard Pass in the Pennine Alps. We visited this establishment when we toured through the Alps while visiting Switzerland, Germany, and Italy. It is a very beautiful and tranquil spot. The monks told us the St. Bernard dog breed was created at the hospice by crossbreeding dogs. The first definite mention of the breed was in 1709. The breed was originally raised to provide guard dogs for the hospice, before they became mountain rescue dogs.

They told us all about the most famous rescue dog, Barry. Barry was a dog of a breed that was later called the St. Bernard who worked as a mountain rescue dog in Switzerland for the hospice. He predates the modern St. Bernard and had a lighter build than the modern breed. He has been described as the most famous St. Bernard, as he was credited with saving forty to one hundred lives during his lifetime. The story goes that Barry's most famous rescue was that of a young boy. He found the child asleep in a cavern of ice in a spot unreachable by people. After sufficiently warming up the boy's body by lying down beside him and licking him, which was the usual way of rescuing a person, he somehow maneuvered the boy around until he had him on his back and carried the child back to the hospice. The child survived and was returned to his parents, although other sources say the boy's mother died in the avalanche that trapped the boy.

After twelve years of service at the monastery, Barry was brought by a monk to Bern, Switzerland, where he lived out the rest of his life. Barry died at the age of fourteen, and his body was passed into the hands of the Natural History Museum of Bern. Following his death, a taxidermist for the museum preserved the body. We had the opportunity to take a photo of Barry when we visited this beautiful museum.

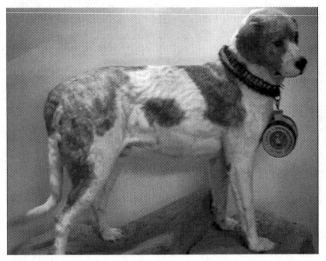

**Barry**

Until September 2004, 18 dogs could still be found at the hospice at any one time. The foundation Barry du Grand St. Bernard was founded to establish kennels in a village further down the path from the hospice, to take over the breeding of St. Bernard puppies from the Friars. I understand around 20 puppies per year are born at the foundation to this day.

The classic St. Bernard looked very different from the St. Bernard of today because of crossbreeding. The Monks told us the winters from 1816 to 1818 led to an increased numbers of avalanches, ultimately killing many of the dogs used for breeding while they were performing rescues. In the 1850s.in an attempt to preserve the breed, the remaining St. Bernards were crossed with Newfoundland's brought from the colony of Newfoundland. As a result, they lost much of their use as rescue dogs in the snowy climate of the Alps because the long fur they inherited would freeze and weigh them down.

**10. Dogs can be trained to be herding dogs.**

A herding dog is a type of pastoral dog that either has been trained in herding or belongs to breeds developed for herding. Their ability to be trained to act at the sound of a whistle or word of command is renowned throughout the world. Collies are recommended as herding dogs.

In Australia, New Zealand, and the United States, herding dogs are known as working dogs, irrespective of their breeding. Some herding breeds work well with any kind of animal; others have been bred for generations to work with specific kinds of animals and have developed physical characteristics or styles of working that enhance their ability to handle these animals. The usual animals dogs are used to herd include cattle, sheep, goats, reindeer, and sometimes poultry.

The term *herding dogs* is sometimes erroneously used to describe livestock guardian dogs, whose primary function is to guard flocks and herds from predators and theft, but they lack the herding instinct. Although herding dogs may guard flocks, their primary purpose is to move them; both herding dogs and livestock guardian dogs are called, for the lack of a better term, "sheepdogs".

Australia has the world's largest cattle stations and sheep stations and some of the best-known herding dogs. We have been very fortunate to see many of them in action.

Dogs work animals in a variety of ways. Some breeds, such as the

Australian cattle dog, typically nip at the heels of animals (for this reason they are called *heelers*). When we first got our present dog, Shotzy, a cross between an Australian cattle dog and a German shepherd, she would nip at people's heels. I guess it is a natural trait for that breed.

Other breeds, notably border collies, get in front of the animals and use what is called *strong eye* to stare down the animals; they are called *headers*. The *headers,* or fetching dogs, keep livestock in a group. The *heelers,* or driving dogs, keep pushing the animals forward. Typically, they stay with the herd.

We have been fortunate to have traveled to Australia and New Zealand twice and have stayed with families on sheep ranches. We have even taken part in going out and rounding up sheep with the farmers, who have used both types of dogs. What these dogs do is truly amazing.

When we flew into New Zealand looking out the airplane window, it seemed like the whole landscape was all golf courses. However, upon landing we found out the very green fields come from all of the sheep in the pastures keeping the grass "mowed" close to the ground. There are more sheep than people in New Zealand. A traffic jam in New Zealand is a herd of sheep going down the middle of the road; as you can see in the following photos, we were caught in a couple of them.

It is such fun watching the dogs working with the sheep. The barking dogs, or the heelers, are driving the herd, and the eye dogs, or headers, are ahead of the flock guiding them in the direction that the shepherd wants them to go. The eye dogs don't bark at the sheep; they stare at them until the sheep go the way the dog wants them to go. We have seen the eye dogs go to the head of a flock by running across the backs of the sheep; it is quite a sight to see.

We also attended sheepdog trial events where the dogs had to corral the sheep, and take them over sort of an overpass; around several objects, fences, through gates, and enclosures; and into a holding pen, as directed by their handlers.

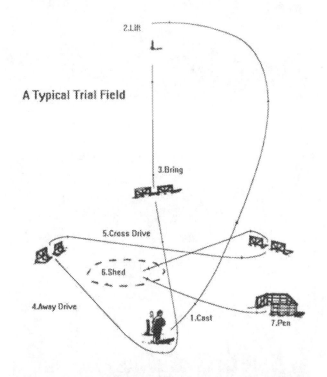

A Typical Trial Field

Our host explained the basic herding dog commands:

- **Come-bye** or just **bye**—go to the left of the stock or clockwise around them.
- **Away to me**, or just **away**—go to the right of the stock, or counterclockwise around them.
- **Stand**—stop, although when said gently may also mean slow down.
- **Way, (lie) down,** or **sit**—stop.
- **Steady** or **take time**—slow down.
- **Cast**—gather the stock into a group. Good working dogs will cast over a large area.
- **Find**—search for stock. A good dog will hold the stock until the shepherd arrives. Some will bark when the stock have been located.
- **Get out** or **get back**—move away from the stock. Used when the dog is working too close to the stock, potentially causing the stock stress. Occasionally used as a reprimand.
- **Hold**—keep stock where they are.
- **Bark** or **speak up**—bark at stock. Useful when more force is needed, and usually is essential for working cattle and sheep.
- **Look back**—return for a missed animal.
- **In here**—go through a gap in the flock. Used when separating stock.
- **Walk-up, walk on,** or just **walk**—move closer to the stock.
- **That'll do**—stop working and return to handler

These commands may be indicated by hand movements, whistles, or the voice. In the trials we watched, they usually used their whistles. Many other commands are also used in working stock.

I would imagine dogs could be trained to herd any other type of animal, but these pictured above are the ones that are most popular, and the ones we observed.

## 11. Livestock guardian dogs.

Another service dog with which we became acquainted in Australia and New Zealand was the livestock guardian dog. A livestock guardian dog is a type of dog bred for the purpose of protecting livestock from predators. Livestock guardian dogs stay with a group of animals they protect as a full-time member of the flock or herd. Their ability to guard their herd is mainly instinctive, as a dog is bonded to the herd from an early age. Unlike the often smaller herding dogs that control the movements of livestock, livestock guardian dogs blend in with them, watching for intruders within the flock. The mere presence of a guardian dog is usually enough to ward off some predators. Livestock guardian dogs will confront predators by vocal intimidation (barking) and displaying very aggressive behavior. These dogs may attack or fight with predators to protect a flock, if they are not able to drive predators off by other means. Livestock guardian dogs may actively look for predators within protected territory to catch and destroy them, and cases are known of dogs luring coyotes to the source of food to hunt them.

The dogs are usually introduced to livestock as puppies so they "imprint" on the animals. This imprinting is thought to be largely olfactory and occurs between three and sixteen weeks of age. There are many myths in the West regarding the training of livestock guardian dogs, particularly the very incorrect idea that human contact should be kept to a minimum. Training requires regular daily handling and management, preferably from birth. A guardian dog is not considered reliable until it is at least two years of age, as before that it is still a puppy. Up until that time supervision, guidance, and correction are needed to teach the dog the skill and rules it needs to do its job. Having older dogs that assist in training younger dogs streamlines this process considerably.

Livestock guardian dogs are generally larger and more protective than other types of dogs, which can make them less than ideal for urban or even suburban living. Nevertheless, despite their size, they can be gentle and make good companion dogs, and they are often protective toward children. If introduced to a family as a pup, most livestock guardian dogs are as protective of the family as the working guard dog is of its flock. In fact, in some communities where livestock guardian dogs are a tradition, the runt of a litter is often kept or given as a household pet, or it is simply kept as a village dog without a single owner.

At least two dogs may be placed with a flock or herd depending on the size of the flock or herd, the type of predators, their number, and the intensity of predation. If predators are scarce, one dog may be adequate, though most operations usually require at least two dogs. Large operations (particularly range operations) and heavy predator loads will require more dogs.

The three qualities most sought after in livestock guardian dogs are trustworthiness, attentiveness, and protectiveness: trustworthy in that they do not roam off and are not aggressive with the livestock; attentive in that they are situationally aware of threats by predators; and protective in that they will attempt to drive off predators. Dogs, being social creatures with differing personalities, will take on different roles with the herd and among themselves. Most stick close to the livestock; others tend to follow the shepherd or rancher when one is present, and some drift farther from the livestock. These differing roles are often complementary in terms of protecting livestock, and experienced ranchers and shepherds sometimes encourage these differences by adjustments in socialization technique so as to increase the effectiveness of the group of dogs in meeting specific predator threats. Livestock guardian dogs that follow the livestock closest assure that a guard dog is on hand if a predator attacks, while livestock guardian dogs that patrol the edges of the flock or herd are in a position to keep would-be attackers at a safe distance from the livestock. Those dogs that are more attentive tend to be more alert than those that are more passive, but perhaps also more trustworthy or less aggressive with the livestock.

While livestock guardian dogs have been known to fight to the death with predators, in most cases predator attacks are prevented by a display of aggressiveness. Livestock guardian dogs have been known to drive off predators that physically they would be no match for, such as bears and even lions. With the reintroduction of predators into natural habitats in Europe and North America, environmentalists have come to appreciate livestock guardian dogs because they allow sheep and cattle farming to coexist with predators in the same or nearby habitats. Unlike trapping and poisoning, livestock guardian dogs seldom kill predators; instead their aggressive behaviors tend to condition predators to seek unguarded (thus nonfarm animal) prey. In northern Arizona we have many ranchers who lease land near and in the national forests, which makes the use of guardian dogs a must, as they are in the territory of many predators. Usually these dogs are larger dogs who put up quite a fuss when predators are in the vicinity, so they coexist quite well.

## 12. Dogs can be trained to be hunting dogs.

A hunting dog refers to a canine that hunts with or for humans. Several types of hunting dogs have been developed for various tasks. The major categories of hunting dogs include hounds, terriers, dachshunds, cur type dogs, and gun dogs. Among these categories further divisions can be made based upon the dogs' skill.

Some dogs are used chiefly for retrieving and flushing game in thick grass or underbrush. These dogs include springer spaniels, Labrador retrievers, the slightly smaller Welsh springer spaniel, and the field-bred American and English cocker spaniel. Brittany spaniels, having working habits close to those of the later developed pointers, are also used. Cocker spaniels are generally used for thick prickly brush that they can duck, dive, and dodge in pursuit of smaller game like rabbits. An uncle of mine owned two very well-trained Irish setters he used to hunt pheasants and ducks. They were amazing to watch.

**American Water Spaniel**

The American water spaniel, Irish water spaniel, and Boykin spaniel are noted for their water work and do very well in temperate water, with the last being adapted to subtropical swamps. They fall into the water spaniel category. Many of these breeds vary their game according to the desires of the hunter: American water spaniels are known to be able to go after animals as big as a large goose in the water or the much smaller prairie chicken out of the water. Both spaniels have a coat more closely adapted to the warm temperatures of the American South, whereas Irish water spaniels are adapted for cool, damp conditions … hence the curly coat and a whiplike tail of the latter.

**Bloodhound (Scent hound)**

Like the spaniels, hounds generally fall into two types: sight hounds and scent hounds. The scent hounds are the younger of the two classes. Typical examples of the scent hound family include the beagle, bloodhound, and members of the coonhound family. There is a great variety in how this group operates, but the one constant is that they have the strongest sense of smell. Coonhounds were originally bred in the American South. They are used to this day to hunt many different kinds of beasts, ranging in size from the squirrel to the American black bear, so accordingly they are bred for great stamina in varying terrain, on water, and on land (all are excellent swimmers); a loud, booming bark that can carry for miles; and a short coat that pairs well with a humid subtropical climate. Beagles have been bred since at least the sixteenth century as rabbit and fox hunters who will relentlessly pursue the scent of prey, even when it goes to ground. These hunting dogs were originally intended to work in large packs—they have a gregarious temperament.

**Saluki (Sight hound)**

Sight hounds, on the other hand, are different from scent hounds in their methods and adaptations. The long, lean head of the sight hound gives it a greater degree of binocular vision, and the body is usually quite slender with an elongated lower spine, giving it a double suspension gallop when it runs. In many cases this class is older than the scent hound group: the greyhound, the Scottish deer hound, and the Saluki have origins going back into the Middle Ages and earlier. Their speed, agility, and visual acuity are particularly adapted for coursing game in open meadows or steppes, and all of them are adapted for running down prey rather than just sniffing for them until they catch up. They are independent in nature and are worked singly or in a "brace" of two or three dogs. Sight hounds are generally quiet and placid dogs compared to other hunting breeds, but they are capable of explosive speed. Rhodesian ridgebacks are one of the few hound breeds with both capabilities, and though they are not the fastest runners they are notable for having exceptional endurance.

**Pointer**

Setters and pointers hunt over long distances to find game birds, like members of the pheasant and quail families, using their noses to find the prey and then sneaking up on them in the brush, showing the hunter exactly where the birds are hiding. Most of this family comes from Europe and would include the shorthaired, wirehaired, German pointers, and Weimaraner, from Germany. Many in this group share traits with spaniels in terms of the coat: it is easier to pick out bits of nettle from a long coat than a short one, and the coat itself offers some protection from damp and thorny conditions.

**Labrador Retriever**

Water dogs fall into two categories: the retrievers and multipurpose. Retrievers are excellent swimmers with characteristic web feet, and they derive from Canadian, American, or British stock. Retrievers typically have oily coats that help repel icy water, and the dogs are noted for having high intelligence and for being very strongly bonded to their masters. Golden retrievers are originally from Scotland: their long, flowing double coats make them ideally suited to Scotland's rainy/wet climate, and their patience on land and in water is the stuff of legend; they will wait for birds for hours and will obey their masters so long as their masters reward them with fond affection. Chesapeake Bay retrievers, very popular in the United States, are bred to jump in the water after ducks and geese even when there is a coating of ice over the water. They have deep chests that act as a jackknife and cut through the ice when they swim. Most famous of all is the Labrador, native to an island in Maritime Canada but popular around the world: the field-type Labrador has longer legs and a slimmer frame than the show type that is better known in Britain, but both show signs of being attracted to water from puppyhood.

**Standard Poodle**

Other water dogs are multipurpose. Standard poodles fall into the water dog category because they originally were used by wealthy Germans to hunt ducks; they predate most types of water dogs. Today there are kennels in the United States that have revived the breed for this purpose, with some dogs proving adept hunters at flushing bobwhite quail and common pheasant and achieving very high ranks in competitions, sometimes beating the more popular Labrador retriever. They are highly intelligent, second only to border collies in overall aptitude, and hunters must be very specific in indicating what they want when giving commands: they cannot be trained by conventional means and require very concrete signals to indicate what is desired so they may solve the puzzle themselves. They are excellent swimmers whose coat requires a simple bath after a swim and a simple cut about an inch off the skin rather than the impractical show clips.

**Portuguese Water Dog**

Portuguese water dogs are medium-sized dogs who will retrieve just about anything from the water and have a strong instinct to swim. Plus they will guard whatever quarry a hunter keeps; they are one of the only water dogs that were bred to hunt fish.

Terriers were bred to kill, and they are among the few hunting dogs that have worked in urban environments: many terriers of English, Scottish, and Irish extraction were extremely popular for killing vermin. Unlike many other hunters, this group did not exclusively work in rural areas. Rats were rampant in Victorian era London, and in Edinburgh, Cardiff, Dublin, Birmingham, Belfast, and Glasgow, and poisons had a marginal effect on them. The rats multiplied in the dirty conditions of the cities faster than traps could be laid. It became very profitable for working-class men to have a profession in which they trained small dogs to sniff out and kill as many rats as they could, as fast as they could. My uncle lived on a farm in Wisconsin, and each year when the corn crib was empty he would move the crib from its usual spot. When he moved it, the rats would run all over the place, but his little rat terrier would kill them as fast as he could. Not many got away.

**Fox Terrier**

In fox hunting they are often paired with hounds should prey go to ground, since most breeds of terrier will pull the fox out of its hole and never back down until its master calls it off. Members of the bull terrier subfamily are used in the United States and Australia for the hunting of feral pigs. Often paired with scent hounds, their job is to wait until the hounds have found the pig and thereafter to charge at it in an explosion of strength and stamina, throwing themselves at the pig and keeping it busy until the hunter comes to kill it. They are bred to have great courage and lightning-fast reflexes, protecting their master and the other dogs from the sharp tusks of an adult boar, and the bulldog blood of their ancestors whispers to them to bite down and never let go.

When I was a kid, my folks had a fox terrier (in the prior picture). My mother never really liked dogs, but she fell in love with Trixie, and she was her dog from the word go. She was a great little dog. She was very loyal, would never leave the premises, and was always curled up around my mother's feet as we sat in the living room at night. When it was time to go to bed, we three boys would go upstairs with Trixie following us. She would lie on one bed or the other, and in the middle of the night if she got cold, she would come to the head of the bed and with her nose would burrow herself under the covers clear down to our feet. The bed was hers, after all, and if we moved during the night and happened to touch her or kick her, we would hear a loud growl.

One story about me and Trixie still haunts me to this day. As Trix got older, she developed cancer and began to deteriorate. I was visiting home from where I lived out of town, and Mom said, "I think we should put Trixie out of her misery, as she isn't enjoying life any longer."

So I said, "I will take her down to the vet right now." And I did. But by the time I wandered around town a little and got home about an hour later, there sat Trixie on the back porch. She had used her nose to raise the garage door of the vet's hospital and found her way home.

Mom said, "This must be what God wants, so I think we'd better just keep her." I didn't listen to her and took Trix right back to the vet's. I am sorry to this day that I didn't leave her with Mom.

## 13. Dogs can be trained to be show dogs.

A show dog might refer to any dog entered into a dog show. More specifically, a show dog is a dog that has been specially bred, trained, and/ or groomed to conform to the specifications of dog shows so as to have a chance of winning a prize. Often used as a single word (*showdog*), the term is also used within the sport of conformation to refer to a dog that displays a particularly energetic or outgoing character.

Entry into many sorts of dog shows is restricted to purebred dogs registered with the kennel club or breed club sponsoring the show, and dogs are selected by breeding to excel at a particular characteristic. However, I understand now that the American Kennel Club is accepting non-purebred dogs in their dog shows.

Dog shows may be held indoors, in horse arenas or other suitably large spaces, or outdoors on groomed fields. Events vary in the requirements for entry and the amount of preparation required. Types of dog shows include the following:

- Fun shows: Usually put on by charities for fund-raising, these dog shows may offer prizes for costumes or for the largest and smallest dogs entered.
- Tests and trials: These dog shows display a dog's training or natural instincts. They may require a great deal of formal training of the dog, as in obedience trials, or none at all, as in herding tests. Some are entertaining spectacular dog sports, such as disc dog and dock jumping, and others are of more interest to the dog than to spectators, as in earth-dog trials and tests.
- Conformation shows: Originally devised for the selection of breeding stock, conformation showing has evolved into a sport requiring specific training for both the dog and the handler, as well as precise grooming requirements (depending on the breed being shown).

We have a close friend who raises Cavalier King Charles spaniels and has had great success in showing them in dog shows, coming up with several grand champions. However, I personally am not a lover of dog shows, because kennel club requirements that breeding be conducted within a breed is tantamount to mandatory, causing continuous inbreeding, as all members of the same breed are related. Another criticism is that whether breeding primarily for appearance or for particularly desirable working styles, too much emphasis is placed on breeding from the few winning stud dogs, causing an already limited gene pool to encounter a genetic bottleneck. A third reason is that I do not believe it is fair to the dog to go through all of the grooming and training for dog shows. I have no statistics, but I also believe that dogs that are bred for show do not live as long as other dogs.

We have owned a Cavalier King Charles spaniel from these champions, but only as a pet. They make a terrific pet, very loving and loyal. However, perhaps because of the inbreeding to make champions, she died of a heart attack at the age of eight years. It was a great loss at such a young age.

14. **The final category is dogs that can be, and are, just plain pets, which to me is the most important category of all.**

In our married life we have had seven dogs, three of which were purebreds. Pet dogs are extremely loyal to the family in which they find themselves. They are truly man's best friend. They will listen to you and not talk back; they will do almost anything you ask them to do. You can be hurtful to them (which I certainly do not condone), and they will still come back to you, lick your hand, and wag their tail. They are great companions and all-around good buddies.

## CHAPTER 6

# Why Children Should Have a Dog

I firmly believe a dog should be a member of the family. The dog can teach a child confidence, manners, and friendship, as well as be a guardian to that child.

The following are pictures of why children need a dog. I think they are adorable. Also, take a good look at the children's faces and the faces of the dogs. They have total trust, affection, and, above all, unconditional love.

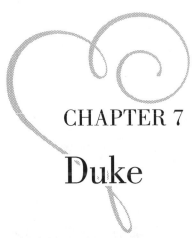

# CHAPTER 7

# Duke

Now I would like to take a few chapters to tell you about the fantastic animals we have had over these many years.

Our first dog after we were married was a boxer, whose AKC registered name was Count Hans Von Stauffenhousen, but we called him Duke. We got him in California as a Christmas gift to our son, Dan. Duke was a wonderful dog.

Shortly after we got Duke, we left him alone in the house while we went to a Christmas party at my brother's home. When we got back home, the Christmas tree was lying on the floor and Duke was nowhere to be found. We looked and looked, and finally Inez looked under our bed and all she could see were two huge brown eyes looking back at her. Evidently when the tree fell over, one of the Christmas ornaments broke and made quite a noise, which must have scared him half to death.

Duke grew to be a very large and powerful dog. He weighed nearly one hundred pounds and was all muscle. He loved bicycle tires. I would take all of the wires out of the bead of old bicycle tires and then give the tire to Duke. Our son Dan would lie on the ground and take hold of the bicycle tire, and Duke would have the other side of the tire in his mouth and would pull him all over the yard. If you held on to the tire when Duke shook his head, it would almost pull your arms off.

It didn't take long for us to understand why that breed is called "boxer": he would stand on his back feet and flay his two front legs just like a boxer. When the legs hit you, it felt like being hit by a baseball bat.

I would put on roller skates and hold on to his leash, and he would pull me all over the neighborhood. Unfortunately, we would be going lickety-split down the sidewalk in front of our house, and he would turn into our house; I wasn't able to make the turn fast enough, and I would go cart-wheeling across the yard, much to the amusement of Inez and the kids.

Duke was a very beautiful dog. He was fawn colored with a white blaze between his ears, on his chest, and on all four feet. I am sure we could have developed him into a champion show dog, but that was not why we had him. He was to be our son's pet.

One day he was in our backyard, which was totally enclosed with a six-foot block wall fence, when some kids were going by on their way home from school. He let out a bark that sounded like he was in a barrel, and the kids barked back at him. He jumped up on the fence and was looking straight down at them; one kid said, "Let's get out of here!" I am sure they thought he must have been at least seven feet tall, but in essence he was only hanging on the fence by his front legs. He would do this by the hour. Besides, he was a very gentle dog and wouldn't hurt anyone unless he or she was trying to do something bad to any one of us; his family.

I was working in the front yard one day, and Duke jumped the six-foot fence and landed right beside me. I lifted him up and threw him back over the fence. He just stood there and looked at me as if to say, "What happened?" He never did try to jump the fence after that.

One evening when I was out of town, Duke was in the house with

Inez and the kids, when someone knocked on the door. As usual, Duke answered with a very deep bark. When Inez opened the door, a salesman was half way back to the street. I am sure he didn't want anything to do with a dog that sounded like that.

One of the things I have found with all our dogs is that if we did something they didn't like, —perhaps going away from the house for a short while or something similar, especially when they thought they should go along or be involved in some way—they would turn to mischief and let you know they were displeased. It is probably due to separation anxiety. Duke's mischief was chewing the electric wires off our hot-water heater's controls, thus causing the heater to go out. Regardless of what we tried to do to prevent it, he did this time and time again. It's a wonder he didn't electrocute himself.

Duke was very disciplined. He knew he was not allowed anywhere in the house except the kitchen, unless he was invited to come into the other rooms. He would lie on the kitchen floor with his legs jutting into the dining/living room, and every now and then when he thought we were not looking, he would inch his body a little more into the room. All we would have to say was "Duke," and he would back into the kitchen with a sullen look on his face. He was an extremely intelligent dog. I never took him to obedience school, but I taught him many things. I took him around our front yard and explained to him where the boundaries were. I only had to show him twice, and after that he would go to the edge of the yard and lie down. No one except me could coax him to cross the line. The line between our neighbor's and our yards was an unseen line, as we both had grass and it was just one big grassy front yard, but Duke would go to the invisible line and stop. He never did cross the line, as far as I know.

Duke went through a lot with us. We had a daughter and two sons while Duke was with us. When our daughter was a baby, Duke would lie by her playpen and watch her as she played. Tragically, Sherri, who had become very fond of Duke and, with the help of Inez or me, would ride him around the living room, developed cancer of the nerves (neuroblastoma). She died following an operation to remove an eight-pound tumor from her abdomen. I believe Duke was a godsend to our son Dan, as he was the only one Dan could turn to after the loss of Sherri. Both Inez and I were far too involved with our own grief to be much help to him. Dan would sit by the hour and talk to Duke. He would take him into the backyard and play "pull away" with the bicycle tire. He would also put the leash on Duke and walk him through the neighborhood. They became bosom buddies. We were so thankful that we had him to help all of us through this trying time.

One day I got up in the morning and went out to the kitchen and found Duke lying on the floor in a big mess of feces. He was very sick. I took him to the vet and, after examining him, he told me that this one-hundred-pound dog had developed cancer. It was like hitting me over the head with a club. I could hardly believe it, because he was only seven years old. The vet said he could treat him if I wanted him to, but the cancer was throughout his body; if he treated it in one place, it would show up in another. As much as I loved that dog, I couldn't allow him to suffer. So I had him euthanized. Though I knew this was the loving thing to do, it was a very traumatic event for me. It was especially hard, as we had recently lost our daughter, and now we were faced with losing Duke, another member of the family. Duke's death was especially hard on Dan, as he was his dog and he was so much help to Dan when Sherri died. It was also the first time Dan saw his father, me, break down and cry. I sincerely loved that dog. He was a true member of our family, and it was like losing another child.

# CHAPTER 8

# Tuffy

Some time after Duke died, I was traveling though my territory in Southern California as a cutting tool specialist, and a customer told me he had a beautiful, totally white Samoyed that he couldn't keep any longer because he was moving. He asked if I would like to have him. Being a softy when it comes to dogs, I said, "Sure." (I did this without even checking with Inez—a cardinal sin, I found out when I got home). I took him home with me that day. Inez was a very surprised lady when I drove in with this huge white ball of fur in the backseat. I knew that she loved dogs as much as I did and was lonesome for Duke, so I was pretty sure that she would not object.

Tuffy was a good, beautiful, friendly dog, but he was rather short on brain power. I guess today, to be politically correct, one would say that he was "mentally challenged." He hardly knew enough to get in out of the rain. But he was a cuddly companion to our son, who was still in grief upon the loss of his sister and his buddy, Duke, and he gave us no trouble at all. He also took to Dan and followed him around wherever he went.

We hadn't had Tuffy very long before I answered the "call" to go to seminary, which was all the way across the country, from California to Maine (more about this in the next chapter). We knew it would be impossible to take him with us, so we gave him to a farmer who also loved dogs, and who said he would be good to Tuffy and he would have lots of room to roam. We never heard about Tuffy from that time on. Again, it was a heart-wrenching decision and we hated to let him go like that, especially when we only had had him for such a short time, but it would have been impossible for us to take him along. We traveled from Southern California to northern Maine in a fairly small camper, and with a wife and three kids we certainly didn't have room for a large dog. Again, it was the loving thing to do.

# CHAPTER 9

# Ginger

After we had lived in California for over twelve years, and we had two more sons (our oldest, Dan, was born while we lived in Illinois), something happened that changed my whole life, to say nothing about the lives of my whole family. We were sitting around the dinner table one Sunday, and out of my mouth came the words, "Honey, I have to go into the ministry!" She looked at me dumbfounded, the kids thought I was joking, and I just sat there totally astounded. I couldn't remember even thinking about the ministry, and I didn't know where those words had come from. They just tumbled out of my mouth by themselves. We just sat there for the longest time looking at one another wondering, "Where do we go from here?" *After all,* I thought, *I am nearly forty years old. I am way too old to think of going*

*back to school* (I didn't have any college except for a few night courses), *let alone seminary*. I had a great job, a nice home, and a good future. Why would I want to do a dumb thing like go to seminary?

A few days after this event, as if by providence, someone who knew my interest in psychology loaned me a recording by a psychiatrist by the name of Dr. Murray Banks. On the record Banks told of a person who came to him bemoaning the fact that he never went to college and saying that was the reason he had never amounted to anything. Banks asked the man, "Why don't you go to college now?"

The man said, "Good heavens, man, that's out of the question. I would be forty-five years old before I graduated."

Banks said, "And how old will you be if you don't go to college?" The man was astounded to find out that he would be the same age either way.

This was the impetus I needed. I immediately enrolled in night school, and there was no turning back. I finished a two-year associate in arts degree in three years, and then completed a third year at Northridge State College. It was then that I quit my job and we all traveled across the country so I could enroll in the Bangor Theological Seminary, in Bangor, Maine. I was forty years old with a wife and three sons. Talk about trust in the Lord.

The first summer after beginning in seminary, I got a job working at a church in northern Maine doing a summer project while going to seminary. On the way to the church, we passed a farm that had a sign by the road saying cockapoo pups for sale. A cockapoo is a cross between a cocker spaniel and a poodle. Our son Dan, who was now fifteen years old, said, "Can't we get another dog? I miss Duke. I miss Tuffy. I miss having a dog." Dan had not taken well to our move across the country, leaving California and all his friends. In fact, if he could have, I'm sure he would have disowned us. So I thought it would be a good idea to get another dog.

Of course, I missed having a dog too, but I was never brave enough to approach the subject with Inez, especially while I was in seminary. We didn't need another mouth to feed and something else to care for. But when Dan begged to get another, I was all for it. So we turned into the farmhouse to inquire about the dogs. They had the pups in a fenced-in area, and I believe there were six or eight of them. Dan selected a black one that was cute as the dickens. He looked at his mother with pleading eyes, and she couldn't say no. We started out of the driveway with the black puppy, and I was thinking everything was just great when Dan said, "I really wanted that little brown one that was hiding way back in the pen." She was the runt of the litter, but the dog was for Dan, so we turned around again and asked if we could exchange the one we had just purchased for the little brown one. I think they were only too happy to make the exchange, because I am sure they thought they would have a tougher time getting rid of the runt than the other dog.

So Ginger became a member of our family that very day. She was a lovely little dog, full of the dickens, and she loved to romp and play and sleep with the kids. We had a large yard at the place we were renting in Bangor, so there was a lot of room for her to run. She would race around the yard as fast as she could go, picking up sticks or whatever happened to be in the yard at the time.

A year later, when I accepted a student pastorate in Pittsfield, Maine, we moved into the parsonage and little Ginger became acclimated in a hurry. It seemed like anyplace was okay as long as we were with her. That has been true with all the dogs we have had. We had her the whole time we were in Maine (six years), she moved with us to International Falls, Minnesota (nine years), and then to Granite Falls, Minnesota (one year).

After being in International Falls for nine and a half years, I decided to run some workshops throughout the southern part of the country. By this time I had taken several courses in death and dying, and biofeedback, so I wanted to share what I knew with people in the nursing profession. We bought a twenty-seven-foot Itasca motor home and started on our journey. Of course, Ginger went with us. We traveled several hundred miles and stayed in campgrounds in many cities and states as I ran the workshops. Ginger was a very good traveler, and we had a lot of fun with her on this trip. She would make friends with all the people in the campgrounds. Doing the workshops lasted for about a year, when it became evident that financially we could not keep it up. So we returned to International Falls and I applied for, and was accepted as, an interim minister in Granite Falls, Minnesota.

One day before we left International Falls, Inez and I were walking down the road in front of our house, when I happened to look back and see that Ginger was following us. By this time she was blind, and I am sure she was following us only by our scent. I knew then that we were headed for trouble and she wouldn't be with us much longer.

Evidently the people who had lived in the parsonage in Granite Falls before us had had a dog. Ginger could smell that dog's scent and, because she was blind, it bothered her terribly, as she didn't know where that other dog was. She finally became very ill, upset, and disoriented, so we again thought the loving thing to do was to have the dog euthanized, as she was suffering a lot. She was about sixteen years old. This of course was another very traumatic event in our lives, as we loved that little dog beyond measure, and we had had her for so long. She, too, was the epitome of God's unconditional love.

# CHAPTER 10
# Spicy

After Ginger, we did not get another dog while we were in Granite Falls, but when we moved to Arlington, Nebraska, a year later, I saw an ad in the paper that read, "Boxer puppies for sale." By this time, all of our kids had flown the coop and we had an empty nest. I was very lonesome for another "child" around the house, so I talked Inez into going to look at them. We wound up with a beautiful, almost black, brindle female. Spicy was a great dog. We got her rather inexpensively because they raised only show dogs, and Spicy had an offset jaw that would have made her ineligible to be a show dog. They told us we could have her if we promised we would have her spayed and not have any puppies. We never have wanted to breed dogs, so we agreed.

Spicy became our clown. Because of her offset jaw, sometimes Spicy would lie on the floor sleeping and her long tongue would roll out of her mouth. When she awoke, she would walk all over the house with her tongue still hanging out. She was responsible for a lot of laughs.

Our parsonage was right across the street from the church, and when it was time for me to come home, Spicy would stand at the front windows waiting to see me on my way home. Then she would come to the door to greet me. She was a great dog.

Two years later, when we accepted a call to a church in Sun City, Arizona, we thought we had better not bring a large dog to a retirement community, as she probably either would not have been allowed or would not have been accepted in the neighborhood. So we gave her to a parishioner who lived on a farm and loved boxers. After we arrived in Sun City, we found out that we could very well have brought her with us, but I guess it was just as well that we left her with our friends. Their relationship became very close, and they loved her very much. She was not too welcomed by the neighboring farmers, however, as she hated cats and the neighbors' cats began to come up missing.

Leaving her after only a couple of years was very hard for me because I didn't think it was fair to her. As always, it was very hard for me to separate myself from the dog. Even though she was with us for only a very short time, Spicy became one of the family and was much loved by us. She left a big hole in our hearts when we had to leave her.

# CHAPTER 11
# Rusty

After we moved to Sun City, we went for several years without a dog. Then, about sixteen years ago, I said to Inez, "Let's go down to the humane society and just look at puppies that are up for adoption." She reluctantly agreed, because she knew that if we saw a pup that we both liked, we would come home with it. I have to admit, there was a method in my madness: I was sure that she would agree to get another dog *if* I could get her down there to look at them.

The humane society that I am talking about is in downtown Phoenix, and they always have several dogs up for adoption. I saw one that I was particularly interested in. It was an English sheepdog named Higgins. He had so much hair that one couldn't tell which was the front and which was the back end of the dog. To say the least, Inez wasn't too enthused, so we kept looking. She spotted a little cocker spaniel that had just been dipped, which I guess they do to all new dogs in the pound to rid them of any fleas or other parasites. He hovered near the back of his cage sopping wet, and he was obviously not a happy camper. Inez crouched down and stuck her fingers through the cage, and very slowly the puppy came to the front and licked her hand. I thought to myself, *We have a dog!*

It seems that this little puppy had been brought in by people who found him wandering in their neighborhood, and they were afraid he might get hit by a car. The humane society veterinarian estimated that the puppy was a purebred about three months old. We told the attendant that we would like to adopt him, and she said, "He won't be up for adoption until ten o'clock tomorrow morning." I guess they have to keep a dog for a certain amount of time to see if its owner will come in to claim it. We were on pins and needles for the next twenty-four hours in hopes that no one would claim him. We were at the pound a little before ten o'clock the next morning, and the attendant held the dog in her arms until exactly 10:00 a.m. By this time, they had blow-dried his coat and he was a beautiful little puppy. When the time was up, the puppy wanted to show his appreciation or tell the attendant where to get off (I'm not sure which), by piddling all over the front of her smock.

The puppy had a deep-red coat, so we named him Rusty. He was a wonderful, wonderful dog—extremely intelligent, sometimes so much so it was spooky. Many times he knew what we wanted from him before we even asked.

In a very real sense, I believe he helped save my life. About the time we got him, I was suffering from what the doctors thought was a serious heart condition, which, as it turned out, was just a stress problem. The doctors told me to just go home and relax and not work for a couple of weeks. It was during this time that we got Rusty. He was the best medicine I could have had. I would sit on the patio, and he would be running around the backyard, see me, and make a dash toward me and jump up into my lap. Many times I thought I would go over backward as he hit me, as he was coming so fast. I immediately fell in love with this little bundle of joy, and that affection grew tremendously throughout many years. He was always at the door with tail wagging to welcome us home when we had been away, whether it was for a long time or a short moment. He simply exuded the very love of God.

After we got home from the humane society, we held Rusty quite a bit to make him feel at home and begin to bond with us. At night we put him in a cardboard box along my side of the bed. When he whined during the night, I would lay my arm over the side of the bed and put my hand on him. He would quiet right down and go back to sleep. For several months we had him in a dog cage when we were not home, and it doubled as his bed at night. It was not very long before we could leave his cage door open so that he could come and go as he pleased. Many times, if we stayed up late at night either watching TV or reading, we would wonder where Rusty was, and we would find him fast asleep in his bed in our bedroom. For many years he spent the night in his cage by my side of the bed, even though the door was open. He wanted to be where we were. In later years he took to lying either by our bedroom door or by the front door.

When we first got Rusty and took him for rides in our pickup truck, he would lie on the front seat and have his head resting on either my or Inez's leg, which made our hearts just melt for this loving fur ball. Through the years he followed this pattern every time we took him for a ride. When we had to slow down, coming into a town or for whatever reason, he would wake up and sit up to see what was going on. Then when we got back up to speed, he would resume his position lying down with his head on one of our legs and go back to sleep. As he lay there, he would sometimes turn over on his back and look up at me with his beautiful brown eyes as if to say, "Okay, here I am. Now scratch and pet me," which of course I always did. He literally had me wound around his little paw.

Rusty fell in love with our truck. When he heard it start up, he would go to the front door and whine and be anxious because he was afraid he would be left behind. He loved to ride with us wherever we went.

Sometimes he would stay in the truck while we tended to an errand. He would always let us know that we were leaving him behind by either howling or barking for a few minutes. Then he would settle down and sleep on the front seat where I sat. This was his truck, and if anyone got too close to it, he would really let them know by barking and jumping at the window. It was the only time that we ever heard him growl in a menacing way.

When we first took him with us in the truck, each time we came to an overpass bridge that went over the interstate, he would duck way down. It took us a little while before we realized he was ducking so he wouldn't be hit by the overpass bridge.

In 1991 Inez and I opened a thrift shop, with the proceeds over and above expenses going to a rehabilitation ranch for badly abused young girls. One day Inez forgot something at the store, so we took the truck, and of course, Rusty, and went to the store to pick up whatever it was she had forgotten. She was taking a long time in the store, so I locked the doors on the truck—it was very warm, so I left the motor running with the air conditioning on so Rusty wouldn't get too warm—and went in to see what was taking so long. I thought all the time that Inez had her keys with her, but she had left her purse, and therefore her keys, in the truck. Here we were, neither one of us with keys, the truck running, and Rusty inside the truck, and we had no way to get in. We called AAA, and they said they would be right out to open the door. An hour later they showed up and opened the door for us. By this time we were really warm, but Rusty was cooler than any of us, as he was in the air-conditioned truck. He couldn't figure out why we were standing outside and not getting back into the truck. I tried to get him to push the unlock lever on the door panel, but to no avail. So we just waited.

We always took him with us when we traveled with the truck and fifth-wheel camper trailer. He traveled with us from Sun City, Arizona, to Minnesota, Oklahoma, and Nebraska many times, and twice to Maine, where our oldest son lives. He also traveled with us to Florida, Oregon, and Washington, and several times into Canada. Once, we attended a family reunion in Maine on a trip during which we traveled almost ten thousand miles; he went along and loved every minute of it. It seemed that he was game for anything as long as we were with him. Everywhere we stopped, he would make friends with everyone in the trailer park. He was a very loving and beautiful dog. When we first started traveling, he would bound up into the truck with no problem, but in later years he had arthritis so he would put his front paws on the running board and then look up at me as if to say, "Okay, I got this far. Help me up the rest of the way." We also had to lift him up into the trailer, as the steps were too much for him. It was sort of sad to see how this puppy, who had had so much vim and vigor, age to the point of needing help to get into the truck and trailer that he loved so much.

When we were traveling, he would ride in the cab with us during the day, and at night he always slept on the sofa in the trailer. When he was younger, he would jump up onto our bed to wake us up in the morning, or if it got cold during the night, he would come up and lie between us to keep warm.

He loved to play ball with me. I would throw the ball, and he would bring it back to me. Many were the evenings that we played this game inside the trailer. I would throw the ball up onto the bed in the front of the trailer, and he would jump up there to retrieve it. Then he would let it fall out of his mouth so it would fall down to the floor, and he would jump down and come running after it. In later years he gave up the game of fetch. Too much effort, I guess.

During the day when we were traveling and the sun was coming in the windshield, we sometimes put Rusty in the backseat of the truck to shelter him from the sun. Even though he wouldn't like this, he would settle down and sleep for a little while. Pretty soon he would lay his head on the center console, telling us he wanted to come back up in front with us. Sometimes we would ignore him, and he would stay that way for miles—his body on the backseat and his head resting on the middle console. Then we would say, "Okay," and he would jump up to the front seat, wait until we lifted the console, and then lie down, like he was in seventh heaven, and go to sleep.

A few years ago we bought a single-wide manufactured home in Pine Lakes Mobile Home Park in Prescott, Arizona, and he loved to go with us when we went there for the day, or for several days. He loved the screened porch at the mobile home because it overlooked the street and he could see the people taking their dogs for walks and be able to say "Hello" with his barks. Rusty particularly loved the Prescott National Forest, which bordered the trailer park, because we would take him for long walks in the forest almost every day.

Rusty was a very smart and inquisitive dog. He liked stopping in the forest to check out all the different smells. When we came home from buying groceries and set the bags down on the floor, waiting for us to put things away, he had his nose in every bag wondering what we had purchased. He never bothered anything in the bags but was just nosy.

Sometimes at night when we were watching TV, he would come around the corner of the sofa with a sock or something else in his mouth. I am sure it was his way of saying, "Stop looking at TV, and pay attention to me." He loved to chew on cardboard. We would give him the toilet roll cardboard, and he would play with it for a little while, but then he started to chew it up, at which time we would take it away from him. If he was able to hide them before we took them from him, he would. Even after he died, we found toilet roll cardboards hidden all over the house. He never liked squeaky toys. I guess he always thought something inside was being hurt, so he would go to the rescue and chew the toy to pieces trying to "free" whatever was making that noise.

Rusty was quite a critic of my organ playing. I would sit down to play, and he, wanting to be with me at all times, would come in by the organ and lie down. However, he always burrowed himself behind the living room drapes so he couldn't hear as well. I am sure that some of the notes I was playing were hard on his ears; but as Rudolf Bing once said, "Egad, what a critic."

Rusty never wanted to be groomed or bathed, but after we fought with him—Inez would have more water on her than he would on him—he would prance around the house like he was King Tut. Everyone who saw him thought he was a beautiful dog. People would crane their necks to look at him as they drove by while we were walking him. We took him for a walk almost every evening. Or rather, he would take us for a walk.

When we first got him I took him to obedience school and we won first prize for his obedience. The only thing I was never able to teach him well was to "heal." He always wanted to be in the lead checking things out. I believe he wanted to be sure it was safe for his "master" to continue.

He was a brave little mutt. He would actually try to attack much larger dogs if they got too near to us. One day as I was working in the front yard of our home, I heard a terrible commotion in the backyard and Rusty was barking his head off. I tore around the side of the house, and a person who was on the green of the golf course behind our home came over and said, "I have never seen anything like that. Your little dog just chased a coyote out of your yard." He was very possessive of our home and our belongings.

Shortly after we got Rusty, he had to be neutered (one of the rules of the humane society), so he ran around the house with a contraption that looked like a lamp shade on his head for about six weeks. This was to keep him from licking the incision. It didn't seem to bother him any, as he continued to play ball with me, bumping the lamp shade on the doorways as he went through but paying no attention to it.

My wife and I have hosted many tours overseas for over forty years. Luckily, we had some very good friends, Byron and Helen Healy, who had had cockers in the past and told us whenever we were going out of town, for whatever reason, they would be happy to take care of him. This, of course, made us very happy, as we never wanted to put him in a kennel. He became very fond of them and was perfectly happy to be with them when we were gone. They, too, fell in love with him and experienced the unconditional love that he gave.

One time in the middle of the night, Byron and Helen were in bed asleep when all of a sudden something landed on Byron's chest. He turned on the light and found out that it was Rusty's empty water dish. He had become thirsty and seemed to know how to get Byron's attention.

Whenever we took him over to their house, the first thing he would do was tear around the house as fast as he could; I am sure he was showing them that he was back. Helen had a room full of teddy bears, and Rusty would head for that room first hoping that the door would be open. If it was, he would come out to the living room with a small teddy in his mouth. I don't believe he ever harmed any of them. If he couldn't find a teddy, he would come out with one of Byron's socks or something out of their wastebasket. He loved to raid wastebaskets to see what he could find. He seemed to have an affinity to Kleenex and would tear it to shreds all over the house.

The Healys never took a cent for taking care of him, because, they said, he was such a blessing to them. In fact, when we returned from one trip they said they had a proposition to make to us. They said, "Why don't we keep Rusty, and then when we want to go somewhere, you can take care of him." Of course that was said in jest, as they knew we would never part with him. But they did continue to call him their "time-share" dog.

Because we knew they would not take any pay, we always looked for teddy bears for them wherever we went. They had teddies from all over the world. We tried hard to get the unusual and had as much fun picking them out as Helen did when we gave them to her. For instance, they had one from Scotland with the teddy dressed in knickers, long stockings, a tam, and a golf bag over the shoulder. One time we gave Helen one that looked like a monkey. She told us afterward that she had thought to herself, *Why in the world are they giving me this monkey, when they know I only like teddy bears?* Actually it was a bear, but it had a costume that made it look like a monkey. She took that one all over the country showing it off to her kids and others.

Another amusing story of Rusty being at their house is that one day he saw geese out on the golf course and made a beeline toward them. They of course flew, and he looked up and watched them as he was running toward them. All of a sudden he found himself in the lake. He hated water, so this was not an amusing event to him, but it sure was to Byron and Helen. One thing we never had to worry about while Rusty was at their house … they always took as good a care of him as we would and, I am sure, sometimes even better. I know one thing; he got many more treats at their place than he ever got at home.

Byron and Helen were very good to Rusty and always remembered him at Christmas with doggie treats. They would package the treats so that Rusty could open them. He would tear the paper off to get to the treats, and then he would proceed to shred the wrapping paper all over the room. Sometimes I think he liked the wrapping paper more than the treats. Christmas was a big day for Rusty.

On December 14, 2003, we sat up rather late to make several tapes of a program that I wanted to send to our family for Christmas. Then we noticed Rusty had been sick and vomited by the back door. We hadn't heard him at all. When I looked into the living room, he was just lying there watching me. I proceeded to go into my office, and Inez was busy cleaning up the mess. All of a sudden Rusty let out two loud screams like he was really being badly hurt. Both Inez and I ran in to him and found him unconscious. We called the emergency veterinarian clinic, which was only a mile from our house, and took him there. They said they found a slight heartbeat and asked if we wanted to have them perform CPR. We said, "Yes!" but shortly afterward they came and told us that they couldn't make him respond. Rusty had died, evidently from a massive heart attack.

I felt that, outside of my immediate family, I had lost my very best friend. Rusty was my buddy, my pal, a member of my family. He followed me around like a shadow and was always either at my feet or lying by my chair. His death coming so close to Christmas made it doubly hard for us. Byron and Helen, too, were devastated by his death. In fact, they purchased a headstone for him when we buried him in our backyard.

I made the statement after Rusty died that it was enough. No more dogs for me. It was too hard losing these magnificent animals. All of us know that a dog does not have a very long life span, but knowing that doesn't make matters any easier when we lose our best friends.

Then I came across the following anonymous quotation, and it really opened my eyes and my heart, and I knew then that Rusty would want us to do what the quote said. So after our next dog, which was given to us, we again went to the humane society and found another great dog named Shotzy, who is still a member of our family.

### A Dog's Last Will and Testament[8]

Before humans die, they write their last will and testament, give their home and all they have to those they leave behind. If with my paws, I could do the same, this is what I'd ask …

To a poor and lonely stray I'd give my happy home; my bowl and cozy bed, soft pillow and all my toys; the lap, which I loved so much; the hand that stroked my fur; and the sweet voice that spoke my name.

I'd will to the sad, scared shelter dog the place I had in my human's loving heart, of which there seemed no bounds.

So, when I die, please do not say, " I will never have a pet again, for the loss and pain is more than I can stand."

Instead, go find an unloved dog, one whose life has held no joy or hope, and give my place to him.

This is the only thing I can give … [9]

Author Unknown

This short quote is so meaningful to me, it brings tears to my eyes every time I read it. I hope it means as much to you when you read it, and if you are a person who has lost your loving pet, you will do what this dog suggests and share your love with another dog, hopefully from a rescue service or the humane society.

After Rusty died, and we told our friends the Adairs we were so lonely without a dog, Kelley Adair arranged for us to meet a woman who, like her, raises Cavalier King Charles spaniels. She told us that she had a dog who was very shy and could not be shown in any dog show, and if we wanted her, we could have her for nothing. Well, Cavaliers usually bring anywhere from two to three thousand dollars, and she was willing to *give* her to us. That was a no-brainer.

Cassie was about three years old when we got her, and she was absolutely adorable … more about her in the next chapter.

# CHAPTER 12

# Cassie

Well, it happened again. The second time in about seven years we went through the traumatic ending of a loving pet. This time it was our little Cavalier King Charles spaniel, Cassie. She had had her teeth cleaned and seemingly was doing great, when all of a sudden she refused to eat or drink much water. We took her to the vet, and he put her on prednisone to stimulate her appetite. Then one Sunday morning she woke our son by her raspy breathing. He came into our room and woke Inez up and told her how she, Cassie, was breathing. Inez went into the living room to see, took her outside to do her duty, which she did, and brought her back into the house. Inez put Cassie down on the floor, and she collapsed. Inez immediately called the vet. He said he would meet us at his office in about a half hour. We took her to the office immediately, but I believe she died on the way to the office. It happened so fast, and we were devastated. We do not know what went wrong—whether it was her heart or lungs that gave out. The only saving grace was she did not have to suffer. She was wagging her tail just moments before this happened. What a shock!!! She was not quite eight years old and seemingly in very good health according to the many tests she went through before her teeth were cleaned just a week before. We had very heavy hearts at that time, as she was the epitome of a gentle, loving, quiet companion.

As I mentioned in the previous chapter, we got Cassie when she was three years old. The person who raised her for the first three years dealt in show dogs. The problem was that Cassie was extremely shy, so it was impossible for her to be shown or bred. Therefore, the owner was looking for a person or family who would have her spayed and keep her for a pet. We had just recently lost our cocker Spaniel, mentioned in the prior chapter, who was fourteen years old, and a friend of the person who owned Cassie told her that we might be interested in raising her. So a meeting was set up for us to meet Cassie; we fell in love with her at first sight and took her home. Cassie, and many pet items, came with the deal at no charge, just the promise that we would love her and take care of her.

She was a charmer, as you can probably tell by the picture. We had a routine that we went through every day. I got up first in the morning, went out to her cage, and let her out. Then she would go into the bedroom to get "mommy" up. I would take her outside to do her duties. We would come into the house, I would go into the den to read the paper, and she would wait until Inez dropped kibble on the floor before breakfast, while she mixed her dog food with more kibble. When breakfast was ready, Inez would say to Cassie, "Go tell him!" She would come bounding into the den and make a circle around the coffee table, barking as she went. That was the signal that everything was ready and she wanted to eat. I would then come out to the table, ask her to speak, and put her dish down beside my chair. She would gobble her food up in about a minute or two and then look for some treats as dessert. We gave her Wheat Chex for her treats, and she just loved them.

The rest of the day would consist of her lying on the sofa, carpet, or the top of the sofa (her favorite spot) for her after-meal nap.

DR. GENE W. LARAMY

On vacuuming day, all Inez would have to do was to move the dining room chairs into the kitchen, and Cassie would be looking for her ball. Inez was kept busy throwing her ball all through the vacuuming process. Cassie would go fetch the ball, bring it back, and drop it right in front of the vacuum cleaner, where Inez would grab it and throw it again. One day she counted how many times she threw the ball during one vacuuming session. It came up to 184 times. It would take her more time to throw the ball than it did to vacuum the whole house. Cassie loved to chase the ball and bring it back. She especially liked us to throw the ball on our fifty-foot porch. She really loved to play, and we were only too happy to accommodate her. She was a beautiful, loving dog. She never complained. And even on the day she died, there was no whining or any obvious suffering, except for the raspy breathing. She always slept all night long and would be patiently waiting for me to open the crate in the morning to let her out. We miss this bundle of fur terribly.

Again, I said this was it: no more dogs. It is too hard to lose them. On the other hand, we had given her a loving home and a lot of compassion. One has to ask him- or herself if it is fair to withhold this loving home from any given number of dogs that land in the humane society shelters. Even though it is terribly hard to lose pets, at least you have the opportunity to give them a loving forever home.

We were very lucky in that our three boys, a daughter-in-law who works for a veterinarian hospital, and a granddaughter were all here to help Inez celebrate her eightieth birthday, as well as Mother's Day, when Cassie died so unexpectedly. They gave us tremendous loving support, which helped us considerably.

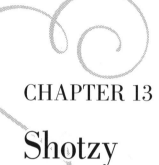

# CHAPTER 13

# Shotzy

**Shotzy**

Following Cassie's death, we were very lonely. So shortly after we got back from a trip to New York and Maine to visit two of our sons, we decided to go to the humane society to see what they had to offer. As you are probably aware, when you walk up and down the aisles of the humane society, all the dogs are barking their heads off trying to get your attention and hopefully find their forever home. On our first day of visiting we saw a little boxer puppy. I have always loved boxers, so we went home to talk about it. We finally decided at our age we probably would not get a puppy. It would be too much to handle, and it would not be fair to the dog. We certainly do not know how long we will be around, and we would hate to adopt a puppy and then not have us around to bring it up. However, when we went back the next day, I still had it in mind to try to talk Inez into getting the little dear, only to find out that she had already been adopted.

So we proceeded to walk the aisles again and hear the cacophony of barks. When we came to this one cage, the dog was not barking but was lying calmly on her little cot. She was a beautiful dog, and we thought the fact that she wasn't barking was a good sign. So we asked to take a look at her in the play yard they have at the society.

To make a long story short, we brought her home with us. She immediately checked to see how far she could go by peeing on the front room carpet. We thought, *Uh-oh, what do we have here anyway?* But she was just checking her limits and never did that again.

Shotzy is an Australian cattle dog/German shepherd mix. When we let our kids know what we got, our daughter-in-law, who works for a veterinarian and also has a dog rescue business, told our son, "That isn't a good dog for them at their ages, as they are so high-strung and will take a lot of attention." Shotzy proved to be the total opposite. She is the calmest dog we have ever had and has the patience of Job. Inez told me, "Maybe you can learn some patience from Shotzy." As I have said before, I am not the most patient person alive that is for sure.

Shotzy has certainly found a home with us. She is just what the doctor ordered. She is lying down beside me as I type this chapter and is sound asleep. She is one gorgeous dog both in looks and personality, and we love her very much. One thing that is different about her than for any other dog we have had is that we can step over her wherever she lies and it doesn't bother her one bit. She is extremely gentle and I think would make a very good therapy dog, as she loves everyone who will pet her and pay attention to her (and, of course, give her a treat).

She was four years old when we got her, and we have had her for five years already. We don't know much about her background, but, unfortunately, she shows signs of having been abused either physically, verbally, or both. She doesn't tolerate loud talking well at all and cowers if I happen to raise my arms swiftly. I simply cannot fathom how anyone can be mean to animals, especially a loving animal such as her. Thankfully, animal abuse is now a felony in all fifty states, and Arizona is one of the strictest of all.

One thing Shotzy does not do at all is play. I sort of miss that, as most of our dogs wanted to play with a ball, a pull toy, or something else. When we first got her, I went to PetSmart and bought myriad toys and brought them home, but she wouldn't have anything to do with them. So I took them all back. I do miss throwing the ball, but that's the way it is. She does love to be with us wherever we are. If we go from one room to the next, she will be right there with us. She loves to go for walks, which we do every morning, and she also loves to ride in the car, which we let her do if the temperature is cool enough. In Arizona the heat can be a real problem. We happen to live in the mountains, which makes it a little better.

## CHAPTER 14

# Interesting Tidbits Gathered over the Years

Many people (estimated to be around two-thirds of pet owners, including me) believe dogs have a sixth sense. Otherwise, how else could they warn their guardians of earthquakes, storms, tornados, and tsunamis (which was very evident in the one that hit off the West coast of Sumatra, Indonesia in 2004 in the Indian Ocean a few years ago when all the animals headed for the hills before anyone knew a tsunami was coming)? They also warn people several minutes, even up to an hour, before a thunderstorm hits. Most say that their dogs become very hyper when a storm or earthquake is imminent.

Scientists have suggested that animals sense bad weather because of changes in barometric pressure or other factors, and they anticipate seizures, low blood sugar, or other medical problems because of hormonal changes, but they haven't figured out what alerts them to earthquakes, bad news, or other events.

I have noticed that our dogs have been very antsy when a thunderstorm is approaching. It could be because of the barometric pressure, or maybe it is because they can hear thunder long before we can.

One woman stated she was awakened in the middle of the night by her dog nudging her. Shortly afterward her phone rang and she received some very bad news. How did her dog know that the woman's father had died at midnight? Other people report their dog just seems to know when there is bad news, when a person is feeling ill, or when their guardians are feeling down.

Then there was a woman who was staying overnight with her mother. The mother's dog was sleeping in her bedroom. The woman told her mother the next morning that the dog jumped up on the bed and on top of her during the night and just about drove her nuts. Her mother asked, "Have you had trouble with sleep apnea?"

The daughter replied, "I have had thoughts about it, yes."

The mother said, "When you stopped breathing is when the dog jumped up on you."

Then there was Rosa, the mine-sniffing dog, who was chosen to receive the Canine of the Year Award from the American Animal Hospital Association. This incredible dog has lived in Bosnia, Croatia, Namibia (Africa), Kosovo, Lebanon, and Cuba, all the while sniffing for land mines and saving lives. Rosa is directly responsible for having cleared over one million square miles of land, returning it to those countries for their productive use.

Another dog got an award for saving his owner. Belle is more than man's best friend; she was his lifesaver. Her diabetic master had a seizure and collapsed. Her master said there was no doubt in his mind that he would be dead if it hadn't been for Belle. His blood sugar had dropped dangerously low, and Belle bit into the master's cell phone to call 911, summoning help. Using her keen sense of smell, Belle determined that her master's blood-sugar level was abnormal. She is trained to periodically lick her master's nose to take her own reading of his blood-sugar level. If something seems off to her, she will paw and whine at him. Her master said that every time she does this, he will grab his meter and test himself. He went on to say, "She is never wrong."

Inez and I used to do a lot of camping. We began in a tent trailer, graduated to one of the first Open Road class C campers, then to a class A motor home, and from that to a fifth-wheel trailer with a Dodge diesel truck to pull it. I say all this because one camp ground we visited had the following slip in the registration form:

> Dogs are welcome in this campground. We have never had
> a dog that smoked in bed or set fire to the blankets in his

camper. We have never had a dog steal our equipment, play his TV too loud, or have a noisy fight with his traveling companion. We have never had a dog that got drunk or broke up his picnic table. So, if your dog can vouch for you—you may stay here, too.

And then there are two puppies, brothers Jeffrey and Jermaine. They were found wandering the streets of Philadelphia. Though both dogs were frightened and sick, Jeffrey had the greater challenge—he was blind. Determined to care for his brother, Jermaine literally became a guide dog. He constantly stayed within touching distance of his disabled brother, and Jeffrey leaned on Jermaine for support. Without any training, Jermaine had become a guide dog. The puppies were always seen touching each other and even slept holding each other. Their story melted the hearts of Philadelphians, and the brothers had no trouble finding a forever home. If animals can be that devoted to each other, shouldn't we be the same? Galatians 6 tells us, "as we have opportunity, to bear the burdens of others." Love is worthless unless it acts out and is expressed in deed and behavior. That's not just puppy love; it's agape love.

In doing the research for this book, I came upon numerous stories about dogs and what has been done to use them and their unconditional love for many different causes. One that is especially poignant is Puppies behind Bars and its offshoot, Dog Tags.

Puppies behind Bars began in July 1997, in the Bedford Hills Correctional Facility for Women—New York's only maximum-security prison for women—with classes commencing the first week in October 1997. Two puppies entered seven weeks later, and by January 1998 five Labrador retriever puppies were living in the prisons being nurtured, loved, and trained by ten female inmates. The prisoners live with the dogs twenty-four hours a day, training them to be service dogs.

At first they were teaching the dogs basic obedience and socializing them to the world-at-large, getting them ready to go into formal training at guide dog schools. The dogs were with them for approximately eighteen months. In 2002 the program was expanded into raising explosive detective canines; these dogs have done everything from "sweep" both the Democratic and Republican presidential conventions, marched up

Pennsylvania Avenue during presidential inaugurations, checked Super Bowl stadiums before fans arrived, and even, sadly, been on hand in the aftermath of the Boston Marathon bombings. The explosive detection canines work all over this country and at US embassies abroad to try to keep us all safe.

From 2002 on, they raised both guide dogs and the explosive detection canines, but in 2006, in response to the number of men and women coming home wounded from Iraq and Afghanistan, they decided to stop raising guide dogs and instead started raising service dogs that they would donate to the men and women who had fought in these wars. They would find, train, and pair the wounded service members with their dogs; in other words, they decided to be fully responsible for all aspects of the dogs' training and their future lives with service members.

They bring the veterans into prison so they can be trained directly by the inmates who are raising the dogs, and they take enormous pride in the follow-up they do with the vets and the dogs for the life of the dogs.

At Puppies behind Bars, they believe dogs can change lives. The dogs have changed the lives of prison inmates who had built walls around their emotions in order to survive in prison. They have helped prisoners learn to love again, and to learn to look at themselves and what they did wrong ... and all-in-all changed the prisoners' lives immensely. The dogs have also changed the lives of law enforcement agents who look for hidden explosives, because the noses of their canine companions are the surest way to find something. They have changed the lives of wounded war veterans for whom, in many cases, war had grown to feel normal, while being home felt very scary.

Dog Tags: Service Dogs for Those Who've Served Us, was established by Puppies behind Bars in 2006 to provide service dogs to combat veterans returning home who have suffered a physical injury, including traumatic brain injury or post-traumatic stress disorder.

Labrador retriever puppies are raised and trained in prison from the age of eight weeks until they are ready to be placed with a veteran. Usually, when the dog is between twenty and twenty-eight months of age, it is matched with a disabled veteran. Puppies behind Bars flies veterans from across the country to New York State, where they are paired with their service dogs and train with them for sixteen days. Currently, approximately fifty service dogs are being trained in four prisons in New York. The service dogs learn ninety-two commands that are standard in the industry (e.g., retrieving objects, turning off and on lights, opening doors so wheelchairs can pass through), as well as twelve specific commands to assist our wounded warriors returning with post-traumatic stress disorder and traumatic brain injuries.

In the Puppies behind Bars spring newsletter in 2013, there was a very poignant story about the love of Sgt. Zoe. The first paragraph reads,

> It's not hard to guess how a young American serving in Afghanistan feels when he or she sets eyes on a small Black Lab. But when Puppies Behind Bars talks to the chaplain about Sgt. Zoe—who was raised by inmates in the Puppies Behind Bars program at Bedford Hills prison officially commissioned by the military and deployed to Bagram Air Base with the chaplain last spring—the impact of the dog in a far-off war comes vividly and powerfully home.

The chaplain goes on to say, "Zoe gives a sense of God's unconditional love to soldiers facing prolonged deployment and combat. Approximately half of the soldiers' families own pets, and a vast majority consider them part of the family. Zoe brings that piece of home to the soldiers."

The newsletter goes on to tell of many hair-raising experiences for the chaplain and Zoe, and how Zoe brought peace and God's unconditional love to many who were grieving the loss of their brothers, comrades, and friends by IEDs and other tragedies. One soldier said, "I am a firm believer in the program of using animals to help soldiers through difficult times." [10]

We have a program in Yavapai County where veterans from the vets hospital who need someone to trust, someone to care for them, come to the humane society and walk dogs, who also need someone to trust and someone to care for them, every day. To fully understand what an ideal match this is, one has to see them together, the veteran and the dog. When the vets arrive, they're quiet and reserved as they enter the kennels. Needy eyes look at them from furry faces. Each veteran chooses a dog eager to go for a walk. Each duo of lost souls depart for the trail, heads slumped low and feet dragging.

About twenty minutes later they return to the shelter. When they come back, their heads are held high and there's a bounce in their steps. The veterans have brought life back to the dogs. They talk to the dogs, and the dogs respond. One is never sure who is more grateful, but one can be certain that both souls have been energized. Both souls are a little less lost. Several letters from the veterans have praised the program, and some have even stated that the dogs have saved their lives. What a wonderful animal a dog really is. They are just beyond description.

# CHAPTER 15

# Animal Cruelty

One thing I cannot understand is the amount of animal cruelty in America. An estimated 1.5 million dogs are euthanized in America every year. This is absolutely horrible and unconscionable. Why are we so unfeeling? Of course there are also over a million abortions each year, so I guess with that mind-set anything can happen. Why we would destroy the messengers of unconditional love, the only place where you can find this other than with God, is beyond my comprehension.

Yes, it is true, I love dogs, but I also love life … and the longer I live, the more I love it. Our seven dogs have given me more unconditional love and satisfaction than I can describe, because there are no words to describe such a feeling.

Thank goodness there are associations such as the American Humane Association, which was founded in 1877, dedicated to the welfare of animals and children. In 1940 it became the sole monitoring body for the humane treatment of animals on the sets of Hollywood films and other broadcast productions. AHA is best known for its trademark certification, "No Animals Were Harmed," which appears at the ends of films or television credits.

In 1954, Fred Myers, as the acknowledged leader of a group of former American Humane Society staff members, founded the National Humane Society, later renamed the Humane Society of the United States. Under his essential vision, determination, and direction, the HSUS not only survived its first decade, but established itself as a national animal-protection organization that addresses cruelty, which lies beyond the capacity of local societies and state federations.

The break from AHA was rooted in disputes about the ineffectual character of the humane movement in relation to the numerous cruelties perpetuated in the laboratory, in the slaughterhouse, and in the wild. However, it was a specific disagreement over pound seizure—the surrender of animals from shelters and pounds—that precipitated the break. Myers favored a vigorous challenge to the increasingly assertive biomedical research community and its efforts to secure animals from municipal pounds and privately financed shelters with pound contracts or other municipal subsidies. Ultimately, he left the AHA in disappointment over censorship of his writings on the topic. Fred Myers made the following statement, with which I totally agree: "All thoughtful persons recognize that cruelty is an evil that should be eradicated from our society, not merely for the sake of animals, but for our own good. We know that cruelty, whether to animals or men, causes in the perpetrator a moral and cultural erosion that is harmful to the whole society."

Even as Myers strove to build a national organization that would address a broad range of cruelties against animals, he and his colleagues never lost sight of the fact that the local societies and animal shelters were the central institutions of the humane movement, around which revolved humane education, cruelty investigation, sound adoption policy, the promotion of spay/neuter, and other essential functions.

From the start, the HSUS worked to advance the work of local organizations, by providing technical assistance and advice concerning animal control, operations management, the training of employees, and the maintenance of proper facilities. Its broad goals included abatement of the nation's surplus dog and cat populations, the reform of euthanasia practices, and the restriction of abuses by the pet shop and commercial pet breeding trades.

Unfortunately, on December 1, 1963, Fred Myers died of a heart attack at age fifty-nine. Luckily, despite the loss, Myers's foresight to help ensure the continuation of strong leadership softened the impact. The balance of idealism and pragmatism he consistently sought to institutionalize within the HSUS proved a still more enduring legacy. Honoring that vision, the

HSUS went on to become the nation's largest and most influential animal protection organization.

We are so lucky here in Prescott, Arizona, because we have one of the best humane societies in the world. Yavapai Humane Society is the largest animal shelter in northern Arizona, rescuing more than three thousand lost, homeless, abused, and neglected pets every year. YHS provides many life-saving services and programs, which resulted in its ranking as the safest animal shelter in the United States by the national leading animal shelter watchdog, Animal People. YHS's "live release rate" is the highest in Arizona and among the highest in the nation, at 97 percent. Prescott, Arizona, is the most dog-friendly city in which we have ever lived.

The story of Chiclet, a nine-month-old female Wiemaraner, is an example of the love and concern of the YHS staff. YHS rescued Chiclet after she apparently escaped her captor. I say captor because her owner had confined her to a tether for most of her young life, clearly not understanding the breed's need to love and to be loved. When Chiclet was rescued, she was suffering from life-threatening injuries aggravated by a collar deeply embedded in her neck. Her captor had neglected to replace her puppy collar as she grew, causing an agonizing garrote-like constriction that resulted in a gaping wound that could have become fatally septic had she not escaped when she did. It's a miracle that Chiclet suffered no serious psychological trauma from her ordeal. Although she still winces when her new owner suddenly raises his hand, she demonstrates only the playful behavior of a typical Weimaraner.

Luckily, Chiclet has been adopted by people who have had Weimaraners before and have a farm where she has lots of room to roam.

We are very proud of the fact that we have a daughter-in-law who runs an animal rescue mission in Minnesota. She has told us many stories of neglected and abused animals. Interestingly enough, she and her partners in the rescue business visit an Indian reservation in Wisconsin several times a year to neuter and spay dogs. They also rescue dogs from the reservation. Indians, who proclaim to hold animals as sacred, for the most part treat dogs in a very inhumane manner.

The following picture was taken from a recent entry on her Facebook page. My question is, "How can people who consider themselves human beings allow anything like this to happen?" As far as I am concerned, tethering a dog is, in itself, inhumane. What is the sense in having dogs if they are not allowed to be part of the family? This is where the punishment should match the crime, as far as I am concerned. As I have said before, people do not have unconditional love like dogs do, or things like this would never, ever happen. Every day, nine thousand pets are killed in American shelters. What a shame!!

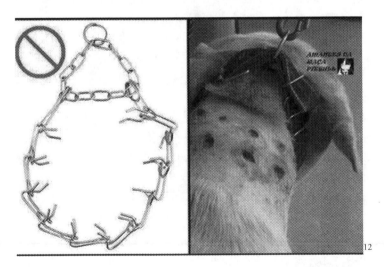

Another act of animal cruelty that most people don't think about is leaving a pet in a hot car. One would be amazed at how hot it gets in a very short time in a closed car, or even one that has windows cracked open. One way to look at it is, would you like to sit in your car, in the summer, with a fur coat on? A canine unit police officer in Phoenix forgot about his dog in the patrol car and left him there for hours. The dog died from being overheated. Of course, many children have also died from overheating in cars while their mother or father was running some errands or, heaven forbid, sitting in an air-conditioned bar. Researchers have proved that the temperature in a closed car will reach 130–150 degrees in about ten to fifteen minutes in the heat of the summer in Arizona.

Letting your dog hang its head out the window as you drive along the road is indeed animal cruelty. A rock thrown up from the tires of the car ahead or a bug flying into a dog's eye going at the speed the car is traveling can cause severe damage to the eye.

Then there are the people who love their dogs to death, literally. Look around and notice how many dogs are tremendously overweight. Dogs should never be given "people" food. They also shouldn't be fed too much. I have seen dogs so fat they can hardly waddle. What a shame. Dogs don't know any better than to eat everything given to them; they trust their custodians to ration food out. Once dogs get overweight, it's almost impossible to thin them down.

Leaving a dog staked in the backyard with a chain or rope connected to it is downright mean. I guess the saying "Walk in the other person's shoes before reacting to him or her" also pertains to a dog. Ask yourself, "How would I like to be chained in the backyard for hours unending without any companionship?"

Kicking or hitting a dog is unconscionable. Again, ask yourself how you would like it. Our present dog was certainly abused either physically or verbally, or both. One can tell by her reactions to different things. Raise your arm real fast, and she will cower. Say the word "No" loudly, which I do quite often if I am watching sports of any kind on TV, and she will leave the room with her tail between her legs, thinking she has done something wrong. One thing we have found is that dogs do not forget being abused, no matter how much love you shower upon them. A person has to be very cognizant of these nonverbals and try not to do the things that bring back bad memories.

Letting your dog ride in the back of a pickup truck is asking for trouble. You may need to swerve violently, which could throw the dog out, causing untold harm. The example of letting your dog hang its head out of the car window also applies here.

Being a kind soul and letting the dog sit in your lap while you are driving is a no-no for many reasons; for example, if the airbag happens to be deployed for one reason or another. It comes out of the steering wheel compartment at approximately 150–200 miles an hour. It could kill your dog instantaneously.

Walking dogs on the sidewalk or a tarred road in the middle of the summer can severely burn their feet very rapidly. Sometimes in Arizona it gets so hot that the macadam on the road is bubbling. Think of what this must feel like on a dog's paw.

There are many more ways to be cruel to animals. Make your own list of the things you see people doing wrong, and then try not to replicate it.

I believe all we have to ask ourselves is what would this thing I am asking of my dog feel like to me, and then govern ourselves accordingly.

Let me be clear—most people do not want to harm their pets, and most do not purposely do so. *They just don't think!!!* Keep in mind you are dealing with a life, a life that loves you with unconditional love, a life that cannot speak for itself. It is you who has a grave responsibility.

# CHAPTER 16

# Parting Thoughts

**If your dog could talk …**

Almost all people who share their lives and home with dogs agree that their animal companions can indeed communicate with them. It's not difficult to understand the signal from a pet that is hungry, frightened, content, angry, in pain, excited, or happy. The communication can be very clear between humans and their pets when they are devoted to one another. Nevertheless, understanding all the needs and feelings of a loving and loyal pet is not always clear. Of course this is especially true in dealing with more complicated issues that go beyond simple physical expression.

What if pets could speak to us? We read many commentaries formulated on this premise. Most are thought-provoking and serve to create empathy and enhance understanding of the bond between humans and their pets. But let us present just a few of the admonitions your pets might present if they could talk to you. Some of the ideas are from unknown sources. You may have seen similar thoughts expressed elsewhere. However, I believe you will agree most are worth considering.

If our pets could talk, they might tell us the following:

- My expected life span is but a fraction of yours, perhaps ten to twenty years. Therefore, any extended separation from you can be painful.
- Give me time to understand what you want of me.
- Please don't tie me to a fixed object in your yard, leaving me alone for hours at a time. I easily become bored and overheated. Being restricted to a small area outside is very uncomfortable for me.

- Please don't leave me outside in the wintertime. I get cold just like you do, and I feel very uncomfortable. I would like nothing better than to be lying inside our home by the fireside.
- Don't be angry with me for long, and don't lock me up as punishment. Remember, I have only you, while you have friends, entertainment, and many other diversions. So please don't leave me alone for long periods of time.
- Before you scold me for my failure to cooperate, please consider that I might not understand what you want or something might be bothering me, over which I have little or no control. Maybe I have a physical problem caused by the wrong food or not enough water, or perhaps it's time for me to visit a veterinarian.
- Should you use corporal punishment to discipline me, remember that I'm capable of fighting back, but I choose not to hurt you.
- Talk to me often. I don't always understand your words, but I do understand your voice when you're speaking to me.
- If you should find it necessary to part with me while I'm still healthy, please make a concerted effort to find me another appropriate home where I will be provided with loving care.
- Please take care of me when I grow old. We will both grow old, but I will age much faster than you.
- When I am elderly and in pain, if I become terminally ill, please don't unduly delay that final act of love to let me go. I know that choosing to end my life is one of the hardest decisions you will ever make. But please don't hold on too long because you can't bear to say good-bye.
- But on the ultimate, difficult journey, go with me, please. Never say you can't bear to watch. Don't make me face this alone. Everything is easier for me if you are there, because I love you.

Love your dog, for your dog dearly loves you with the *unconditional love of God*!!!

If people in this world were more like dogs, we would have a much better world. You just can't get any better than that.

# ABOUT THE AUTHOR

Gene W. Laramy answered the call to the Christian ministry late in life. He graduated from the University of Maine, and the Bangor Theological Seminary, in the same year. He went on to earn his Doctoral Degree in psychology at the San Francisco Theological School. He furthered his studies at the Dr. Elizabeth Kübler-Ross Institute and the Menninger Foundation, as well as many workshops. Dr. Laramy has served churches in Maine; Minnesota; Nebraska; and Arizona. He has conducted workshops on Death and Dying, and Stress Management throughout the United States. He founded and serves as Director of Education for Living, an organization with the purpose of helping people help themselves through education. He and his wife, Inez, have led educational tours for Nawas Int'l Travel for 37 years, traveling to all points of the globe. They have three sons, three grandchildren and three great-grandchildren. He is semi-retired and lives with his wife of 67 years in Prescott, AZ

# ENDNOTES

1    The information about Dogs for the Deaf and autistic assistant dogs is certified to be correct per Blake Matray, CEO of Dogs for the Deaf, and is used with his permission.

2    Dogs can be trained as therapy dogs excerpt and picture of Smoky are © 2014, by William A. Wynne and are used with his permission.

3    Material about therapy dogs written by Nancy Stanley, founder of Tender Loving Zoo, and author of the charming book *Pillow with a Heartbeat*, is used with her permission.

4    The information about Therapy Dogs Incorporated is used with the permission of its board of directors.

5    These fantastic pictures of the 9/11 destruction and the search and rescue dogs were taken by Andrea Booher, photographer and film maker from Aspen, Colorado, and are used with her permission.

6    Pictures of Michael Hingson at the WTC memorial wall, cuddling his dog, Roselle, and the portrait of Roselle are used with Michael's permission.

7    Cartoon picture of a "herding" dog was painted by Inez Laramy and is used with her permission.

8    "A Dog's Last Will and Testament" is used with agreement by Deanna Raeke (*For the Love of the Dog*) who is licensed under a Creative Commons Attribution-Share Alike 3.0 United States License http://creativecommons.org://purl.org/dc/terms/" "http://fortheloveofthedogblog.com/article/dog-writing-

poetry/a-dogs-last-will-and-testament"For the Love of the Dog "http://fortheloveofthedogblog.com http://creativecommons.org.

[9]    This excerpt about Puppies behind Bars and Dog Tags is used with their permission.

[10]   Picture of Chiclet was taken by Ed Boks, Director, Yavapai County Humane Society, and is used with his permission.

[11]   I could not obtain permission to use this picture of the results of using a prong collar, as I couldn't find out who took it. However, I think it is so important to pass on this message to *ban this type of collar* that I insert it here anyway. It has been shown on Facebook and several other places, so I assume it is public domain.

[12]   All Scripture selections are taken from the Revised Standard Version of the Bible, 1952.

Printed in the United States
By Bookmasters